W9-BCY-148

Su Man-Shu

TWAYNE'S WORLD AUTHORS SERIES

A Survey of the World's Literature

Sylvia E. Bowman, Indiana University

GENERAL EDITOR

CHINA

William R. Schultz, University of Arizona

EDITOR

Su Man-shu

(TWAS 191)

TWAYNE'S WORLD AUTHORS SERIES (TWAS)

The purpose of TWAS is to survey the major writers–novelists, dramatists, historians, poets, philosophers, and critics–of the nations of the world. Among the national literatures covered are those of Australia, Canada, China, Eastern Europe, France, Germany, Greece, India, Italy, Japan, Latin America, the Netherlands, New Zealand, Poland, Russia, Scandinavia, Spain, and the African nations, as well as Hebrew, Yiddish, and Latin Classical literatures. This survey is complemented by Twayne's United States Authors Series and English Authors Series.

The intent of each volume in these series is to present a critical-analytical study of the works of the writer; to include biographical and historical material that may be necessary for understanding, appreciation, and critical appraisal of the writer; and to present all material in clear, concise English–but not to vitiate the scholarly content of the work by doing so.

Su Man-shu

By LIU WU-CHI
Indiana University

Twayne Publishers, Inc. :: New York

Library of Congress Catalog Card Number: 70–120494

MANUFACTURED IN THE UNITED STATES OF AMERICA

Acknowledgments

In the preparation of this manuscript I am grateful to Mr. Lo Hsiao-ming for his encouragement and help in securing materials on the author's life and to Professor William Schultz for editing. Unless otherwise acknowledged, all translations are mine.

Preface

The compilation of this critical biography of Su Man-shu, a Sino-Japanese poet, story writer, painter, and revolutionist turned Buddhist, represents the fulfillment of a pledge made in 1943, when the *Memorial Volume of the Reverend Man-shu's Works* was published in commemoration of the twenty-fifth anniversary of his death. As we look back upon the eventful years that spanned half a century from 1918 to 1968, we can assert with confidence that time has not obliterated the fame and influence which Su Man-shu enjoyed during his lifetime. The zenith of his popularity was reached in 1928 when the five-volume *Complete Works of Man-shu*, compiled by my father and myself, sold tens of thousands of copies, a record sale for a Chinese book in those days. Even though it was then the time of the new literature movement with its emphasis on colloquial, realistic delineations of life, Man-shu's romantic literary tales and poems commanded a large following among young intellectuals and influenced their attitudes and general outlook.

For Chinese writers in the first decades of the present century, revolutionary fervor and sentimentality, while seemingly unrelated, were their two main sources of inspiration. Oppressed by the harsh realities and inequities of life, they were motivated by a fervor for profound social and political change; as these hopes were dashed by events, their spirits plummeted to the nadir of distress and despair, engulfing them in waves of morbid emotion. Man-shu's romantic sentiments were well known to his friends, but it was not until the late 1920's that our studies of his life revealed in him a hitherto unsuspected element—a revolutionary spirit, however transient and short-lived, which spurred him to action during his youth. This aspect of his character became even more evident as more facts about his personal history were disclosed by former friends and revolutionary comrades. Needless to say, the failure of his effort to save the country plunged him, as it did many of his friends, into a pessimism and self-abandonment that ultimately led to his premature death.

His contemporaries mourned his early passing, the pathetic brevity of a promising career. A lonely monk, forever on the move, Man-shu was deprived of the warmth of home and family. It is almost tragic that the familial love, denied him by members of his paternal family, was transferred to a Japanese woman whom he recognized, after a separation of almost twenty years, as his long-lost mother! At their reunion, Man-shu had to enlist the services of a former schoolmate as an interpreter, for his Japanese had become rusty after long disuse. On the other hand, it speaks well of the genuineness of his nature that once he had found his mother, he gave her an affection and devotion that was to last until the end of his life.

The greatness of an artist is to be judged not by his ability to arouse in others a sense of compassion for his personal mishaps and sufferings but by the intrinsic worth and merits of his own works. While Man-shu's poetic accomplishments, his storytelling, his craftsmanship, his beautiful literary style, his disarming personality are all praiseworthy, his chief claim to excellence seems to lie in his ability to express with candor and spontaneity feelings of the heart, and just as his life and personal experiences were unique, so are the emotions he evokes in his poems, or vicariously through his heroes, most of whom reveal the personal traits of the author himself. But what provides his writings with their most exciting and lasting qualities is an aura of exoticism pervading his poems, short stories, and the novel, *The Lone Swan.* The last is an intriguing tale of passionate but helpless love that tears apart two young, sensitive people brought up separately in China and Japan but drawn to each other by blood ties and spiritual kinship. No Chinese writer had previously made use of a situation involving dual national origins, or contrasting modes of life of the family and the monastery, to add color and zest to their writings. No wonder, then, that Japanese critics, like their Chinese counterparts, have been impressed by and have highly praised his genius.

One Western scholar has also been attracted to the career of Su Man-shu. I must confess my surprise at the discovery in 1961 of Henry McAleavy's small book, *Su Man-shu, A Sino-Japanese Genius* (1960). I never expected a Western writer to delve into the life and works of a man seemingly so remote from the present. With little material on Su Man-shu's life and times available to him, beyond what he was able to garner from the reminiscences of one of Man-shu's early friends, McAleavy treats his subject as a sort of literary curiosity of some bygone time in an alien land, as one would a little known sixteenth-century British author. Nevertheless, this pioneering study did serve to acquaint the English-language reader with a neglected but important literary figure.

When I resolved in 1943 to undertake this biographical study, I had in mind a work in the Chinese language. But, unable to remain in my native land, it is natural that I should write in the language of the people with whom I have been associated during the past twenty years. The appearance of the McAleavy book stimulated a renewed interest in Man-shu on my part and also reminiscences of my childhood, when I gazed with boyish curiosity upon the strange golden statuette of the Buddha which my father's monk friend had sent us from the South Seas, or the two silk flowers which he once gave me with the inscription "To my female younger brother"—what a kindly insult! There were also those hot, memorable summer days in my freshman year when, inspired by Man-shu's translations of Byron and Shelley, my two favorite poets at the time, I began my study of his life and works. Thus, with my father's help, I published successively in 1927 and 1928 a volume of Man-shu's poems, a reprint of two newly discovered prose works, a chronology of his life, and ultimately the standard edition of his collected works, a joint undertaking of my father and myself. This was to be our first and only collaboration, an occasion to be deeply cherished at this fiftieth anniversary of Man-shu's death, which is also the tenth anniversary of my father's passing! It is fitting that I dedicate to his loving memory, even as I myself have lived more than ten years beyond "the age of knowing my fate," this English biography of one of his most beloved friends as well as one of the foremost Chinese writers at the turn of the century.

LIU WU-CHI

Bloomington, Indiana
1968

Contents

Preface

Chronology

1. Family and Early Life 15
2. A Young Revolutionist Turned Buddhist 24
3. Man-shu and His Literary Circle 38
4. The Wandering Poet-Monk 53
5. The Southern Society and the South Sea Islands 68
6. *The Lone Swan* 83
7. The Journey's End 97
8. An Heir of Unfulfilled Renown—An Epilogue 122

Notes and References 144

Selected Bibliography 153

Appendix I. A Genealogy of the Su Clan 157

Appendix II. A Short Biography of Su Man-shu by Liu Ya-tzu 158

Index 163

Chronology

1884 Born in Yokohama, Japan, on September 28.
1889 Returned to Li-ch'i, Kwangtung province, China.
1896 Went to Shanghai.
1897 Stayed with aunt in Shanghai.
1898 Returned to Yokohama and entered Ta-t'ung School.
1902 Entered senior preparatory course at Waseda University.
1903 Entered Ch'eng-ch'eng Academy in Tokyo; returned to Shanghai; went to Hong Kong, thence to Hui-chou, Kwangtung, and became a Buddhist monk.
1904 Traveled to Siam and Ceylon and started to learn Sanskrit; taught at the Industrial School in Ch'ang-sha in the fall.
1905 Went to Nanking to teach at a military school.
1906 Taught at Ming-te School (Ch'ang-sha) and Wan-chiang Middle School (Wu-hu); traveled in China and Japan.
1908 In Japan, published *Affinities in Literature*; returned to China to teach in the Buddhist Institute (Jetavana School) in Nanking.
1909 In Japan, published *Selected Poems of Byron*; moved to Surabaya, Java, to teach.
1911 Vacationed in Tokyo and published the *Voices of the Tide*.
1912 Left Java for Hong Kong and Shanghai to join the editorial staff of *The Pacific News*; published *The Lone Swan*.
1913 Traveled widely in China and Japan and published *Random Notes from a Swallow's Mausoleum*.
1914 In Japan, published the *Esoteric Essences of Chinese-English Poetry*.
1916 Returned to China.
1917 Extended illness and recuperation.
1918 Entered Kuang-tz'u Hospital in the Shanghai French Concession; died May 2.

CHAPTER I

Family and Early Life

AS China entered the second half of the nineteenth century, a general unrest prevailed throughout the countryside. While still nursing the wounds of defeat suffered in the Opium War (1839–42) with Great Britain, new disasters ensued: armed conflict with England and France (1856–60), resulting in the capture of Peking by the allied forces; the T'ai-p'ing Rebellion (1850–65), which devastated much of the fertile and prosperous Yangtze delta; and the Nien and the Moslem rebellions which raged in the southwest and northwest for more than a decade. Foreign powers threatened to dismember the Chinese empire, while internal disorder reflected growing discontent and a resurgence of revolutionary fervor. Weak, youthful emperors occupied the throne and ambitious court officials intrigued against one another. By the end of the nineteenth century, which saw more foreign invasions and native uprisings, it was apparent that the Manchu monarchy was doomed.

During this period, on September 28, 1884, some twenty years after the fall of the T'ai-p'ing kingdom, the Chinese poet Su Man-shu was born, not in China but in Yokohama, Japan. Like many of his fellow Cantonese, Su Chao-ying (Su Chieh-sheng), the boy's father, had come to Japan to engage in trade. As the manager of the British-owned Wan-lung Tea Company in Yokohama, he was well situated among the local Chinese community. Forty years old when Man-shu was born, his Yokohama household included a Japanese concubine, Kawai-sen, familiarly known as O-sen, age thirty-six, and a Chinese concubine, Elder Ch'en-shih, age seventeen. His legal wife, Huang-shih, age thirty-seven, and his eldest son by Kawai, Hsü-t'ing, age ten, resided in Kwangtung province at the family home. Huang-shih joined him in Yokohama between 1886 and 1889. Two years later another Cantonese woman, Younger Ch'en-shih, was brought to Japan as his second Chinese concubine.

In Japan, where Su Chieh-sheng made his temporary home, the Meiji reformation had been in full swing since 1868. With the establishment of Tokyo as the new capital, Yokohama, linked in 1872 to Tokyo by the first Japanese railway and to the outside world by steamships recently introduced from abroad, assumed even greater importance than before as the country's chief port and commercial center. During the same period, the Meiji government undertook a number of reform measures such as the abolition of feudalism, the codification of the penal law, the revision of treaties with Western nations, and the promulgation of a new Japanese constitution in 1889. All in all, the modernization of Japan, which hastened her emergence as a world power, contrasted sharply with the conservatism of the Chinese empire across the sea. The Chinese communities in Japan, consisting mainly of business men like Su Chieh-sheng, were more interested in making money and raising families than in politics and the international situation. It was not until 1895 that the first group of Chinese students arrived in Japan to sow the seeds of revolution among their compatriots.

The Su clan resided at Li-ch'i, a village of some one hundred households in Hsiang-shan county, Kwangtung province. The most enterprising of their fellow countrymen, the Hsiang-shanese not only migrated to foreign countries in East and Southeast Asia, but ventured even farther east to Hawaii and the United States. A few years before Su Man-shu was born, Sun Yat-sen (1866–1925), also a native of Hsiang-shan, left home for a new life in Hawaii, where he received a Western education. Early contacts with foreigners awakened in the Hsiang-shanese and others a sense of nationalism and revolutionary fervor.

Su Man-shu's grandfather, a pioneer Cantonese merchant, lived in retirement at home with his numerous sons and grandchildren. It was he who started the family's import-export trade with Japan, and his foreign connections helped establish his eldest son, Chieh-sheng, in the tea business at Yokohama. Following in the footsteps of his father, Su Chieh-sheng traveled back and forth between Hsiang-shan and Yokohama, where early in 1873 he took Kawai-sen as his concubine. Two years later she bore his first son, Hsü-t'ing. Between 1877 and 1879, she lived at the Su family home in Hsiang-shan. Possibly it was the birth and upbringing of Hsü-t'ing, the first male heir of the Su clan, that had occasioned her visit, from which she learned firsthand of Chinese life in a traditional family.

Throughout his adult life, Su Man-shu complained bitterly of "the unutterable pangs of his life." At one time it was believed that Man-shu was of purely Japanese ancestry, the son of a Japanese man and Kawai, who after the death of her husband brought Man-shu with her to Chieh-sheng's house. This theory has proved to be groundless, however. Immediate members of the Su family, chiefly Elder Ch'en-shih, who were with Chieh-sheng in Yokohama at the time of Man-shu's birth, have refuted this claim. While Man-shu's ancestry on his father's side is established beyond doubt, questions have been raised as to the identity of his mother. According to the same source, Man-shu's real mother was not Kawai but a a Japanese girl named Owaka, who reportedly left the Su household shortly after Man-shu's birth, and about whom very little else is known. According to information supplied by Elder Ch'en-shih, Owaka was a maidservant in Chieh-sheng's employ. More recent information from one of Man-shu's early schoolmates[1] suggests that Owaka may have been Kawai's niece, and was then staying with Kawai and Chieh-sheng as an assistant in the Su household. This would explain the affinity and warmth which Kawai felt for Man-shu.

Whatever Su Man-shu's parentage, the boy was brought up by Kawai in Chieh-sheng's Yokohama establishment, and she must be regarded, as she was by Man-shu himself, as his mother, at least by adoption. Kawai and Man-shu were separated in 1889 when the six-year-old boy returned with Huang-shih to the Su family home at Hsiang-shan to grow up among his father's relatives, as Hsü-t'ing had done before him. Three years later in 1892, upon the failure of his tea business,[2] Su Chieh-sheng also returned home with his two Chinese concubines. Kawai remained in Yokohama. One account has it that even before his departure from Japan, Chieh-sheng had already severed relations with Kawai. Whatever the case, it is fairly certain that Chieh-sheng never returned to Yokohama, nor did Kawai again visit the Su family home in Hsiang-shan. Some communication appears to have existed between Kawai and Su Hsü-t'ing when he went to Japan in 1895 to learn the family trade from a maternal uncle, Lin Pei-ch'üan. Man-shu himself did not resume his ties with Kawai until much later when he was twenty-four. By that time, Kawai, who was turning sixty, had married an elderly Japanese merchant. Man-shu does not seem to have taken unkindly to her remarriage, which may however have terminated Hsü-t'ing's relationship with her. To Man-shu, Kawai was always a woman of great affection and refinement, and during the next eleven years of his life a close bond existed between them.

On the other hand, Man-shu's relationship with his father was less intimate. After the early years in Japan, father and son lived at Hsiang-shan from 1892 to 1895, and the next year and a half in Shanghai. From then on, father and son went their separate ways and there is no evidence they ever met again. The reasons for Man-shu's alienation from his family are not known. When in Hong Kong in 1904, he even refused to return home to see his father when told of the latter's illness; he also failed to attend his father's funeral in the same year.

Su Man-shu's boyhood at Hsiang-shan lasted for seven years, from 1889 to 1896. Though a long period in his life, these years have remained a blank to his biographers. It is to be presumed that he enjoyed the companionship of his numerous brothers, sisters, and cousins. At school, which he first attended in his seventh year, he began to learn the rudiments of a classical Chinese education typical of the time. The transition from Japanese to Cantonese should not have been difficult since Cantonese must also have been spoken in Yokohama, as it was later in Hsiang-shan. Here little excitement marked Man-shu's life except for such family occasions as his father's return from Japan with his two concubines in 1892, and later his departure with Elder Ch'en-shih for Shanghai in 1895. The Sino-Japanese War (1894–95) would hardly be expected to have created much excitement in the daily routine of a remote southern village, but because of their business connections in Japan, the Sus were probably more aware of the conflict than other villagers. Moreover, the schools of that time were often the incubators of patriotic and revolutionary ideas, and it may be surmised that at the impressionable age of eleven, Man-shu harbored the same resentment that students everywhere felt at China's humiliating defeat by Japan. Very soon, Man-shu himself was to be drawn into the political and intellectual maelstrom that agitated young people in the big cities.

The vista of a glittering metropolitan life greeted the country lad from Hsiang-shan when he left home in 1896 to join his father in Shanghai. This large commercial city had grown and prospered since it was opened as a treaty port in 1842. During the almost quarter century from 1896 to 1918 when he died, Shanghai was a familiar haunt of his, and one that impressed him with its variety of contrasting moods, its gaiety and misery, its dire poverty and immense wealth, its tall buildings and tenement houses, and its broad avenues and congested narrow lanes. It was a city endowed with many amenities of life, such as music, drama, and the other beaux arts; it also festered with the cankers of society—beggary, gambling, prostitution, and opium-smoking. To the new visitor, the ugliness and filth of metropolitan life was often hidden from view by a dazzling and imposing exterior.

The gay, bustling activities in Shanghai may have reminded Man-shu of Yokohama, now fading from memory. There was, however, one vast difference between the two cities. The immense wealth of metropolitan Shanghai was partially controlled by westerners, who found it an adventurer's paradise in which to amass a fortune and to indulge in the manifold pleasures of life. In the foreign concessions were to be found spacious residential areas, magnificent banks, tall department stores, and beautiful parks with tree-lined avenues and green lawns, from which Chinese and dogs were excluded. But these restrictions and inequalities notwithstanding, war-weary and hunger-stricken Chinese from the neighboring towns and countryside flocked to Shanghai for safety and a livelihood. For them the city provided a semblance of peace and order, as well as an opportunity to eke out a meager existence. At the same time, many wide-eyed young men from the interior converged on Shanghai to seek a modern education in its numerous schools, some of them missionary, where they could obtain a firsthand knowledge of science and technology, new political ideas and economic theories, and foreign languages such as English, French, and Japanese. Thus, Shanghai had the distinction of being not only a citadel of foreign enterprise and commerce, but also a center of revolutionary aspirations and activities for China's young intellectuals.

In this city of strange contradictions, Man-shu now found himself. Later, he made it his traveling headquarters as he shuttled back and forth between China and Japan. It was there that he first met those men of letters who were to exert a profound influence on his life, and it was for the Shanghai newspapers that he wrote inflammatory political articles, while at other times enjoying himself with sing-song girls at "flower-and-wine" parties. These episodes in his life belong, however, to the later part of this narrative. Initially, his major preoccupation in Shanghai was to learn the English language, as many did who took up residence in this British-dominated treaty port.

In April, 1897, Su Chieh-sheng was called home to attend his ailing father, who died a half year later. Elder Ch'en-shih accompanied him, while Man-shu remained with his aunt and her husband, until the following year, 1898, when at the age of fifteen he was sent to Yokohama in the company of an older cousin, Lin Tzu-yüan, the nephew of Lin Pei-ch'üan. He joined Hsü-t'ing, now a young man in his early twenties, who had been chosen by his father to succeed him in the family business and who was learning the tea trade in Japan. Fortunately for Man-shu, his family treated him differently. He was given an opportunity to obtain a formal education. Possibly an interest in modern education influenced the Su family to send Man-shu to the Ta-t'ung School, a private institution newly established by the Chinese community in Yokohama for the education of their young members.

The school was named Ta-t'ung, literally "Universal Harmony" or "Great Commonwealth," by K'ang Yu-wei (1858–1927), a colorful Cantonese intellectual then living in Shanghai at the height of his fame as a Confucian scholar and political writer. When the founders of the Yokohama Chinese school went to him for assistance, he not only gave the school its name but also recommended four of his followers as teachers, one of whom became its principal. Established as a preparatory school for the instruction of Chinese and English, Ta-t'ung grew in the course of the next decade into an institution offering instruction at all levels from kindergarten through high school. Its growth, however, was not without trouble, for it had to face not only critical financial problems and the rivalry of other Chinese schools in Yokohama, but also a tense political situation that arose as a result of K'ang Yu-wei's role in the short-lived Reform Movement of 1898.

In that year, K'ang Yu-wei, together with his disciple Liang Ch'i-ch'ao (1873–1929) and others, had gone to Peking as advisor and confidant to the young Manchu emperor Kuang-hsü, who sought to save the empire from disintegration by initiating a series of reform measures. For a period of one hundred days in the summer months of 1898, a succession of edicts ordering sweeping reforms in government were issued. Regarded as excessively radical and dangerous, these measures so alarmed conservative court officials that they rallied under the leadership of the empress dowager Tzu-hsi, who had previously relinquished the reins of government she had held for almost twenty years during the emperor Kuang-hsü's minority. In a *coup d'état* the empress dowager resumed her regency, imprisoned the emperor, and executed a number of reformers; K'ang and Liang barely escaped to Japan.

The repercussions of this political incident were felt among the Chinese communities in Yokohama. Some community leaders, at the instigation of Chinese diplomatic officials, sought to destroy the Ta-t'ung School, which the officials considered to be a hotbed of reformist ideas. The crisis came to a head in 1902 with the invasion of the school compound and the destruction of its properties by a band of hired rowdies. Litigation followed, and the school was sued for failure to pay its rent. At this critical juncture, the one person responsible for staving off the disaster that threatened Ta-t'ung was no other than Lin Tzu-yüan, Man-shu's cousin, at that time one of the school directors.

Man-shu studied at the Ta-t'ung School for four years until he left for Tokyo in 1902. For a new private school, the faculty was quite distinguished. Among the Chinese teachers were four of K'ang Yu-wei's disciples, including Hsü Chün-mien, the school principal. Lu Hsiang-fu, who taught classical Chinese philosophy, was still living in Hong Kong in 1965 at the advanced age of ninety-seven. English was taught by graduates of Queen's College in Hong Kong. A few Japanese instructors were also on the staff, one of whom served as an instructor of military science, a class which Man-shu must have attended. The students at Ta-t'ung organized a baseball team called the Yellow Dragon, to which several of Man-shu's friends belonged, but not Man-shu himself.

The atmosphere at Ta-t'ung was pervaded by a conservative Confucian outlook and fervid patriotism. With K'ang Yu-wei's followers at its helm, Confucius was worshiped every Sunday when students were required to kneel in front of the sage's image, refusal to do so being punishable by expulsion. On the other hand, the pupils were also inculcated with a sense of national spirit and identity. Every day at the adjournment of class, students were asked to chant the following slogan:

Our national humiliation has been avenged,
And the people's life is still full of hardships.
Do not forget it every time you take your meals.
Oh, young men, exert yourselves diligently![3]

These patriotic sentiments must have profoundly influenced Man-shu. One of his classmates has recalled that Man-shu often used to remark that "like the scholars of olden times, one should have no reason to regret the death of a patriot"—a famous saying attributed to the mother of a great scholar who was killed in a struggle with a powerful eunuch faction toward the end of the Later Han dynasty.

Another schoolmate of Man-shu at this period was Feng Tzu-yu (1881–1958), who later attained fame as a historian of the Chinese revolution. His father, Feng Ching-ju, owner of a stationery and printing shop at Yokohama, was one of the founders of the Ta-t'ung School. When Sun Yat-sen fled to Japan in 1895 after the failure of his first attempt at revolution in Canton, he and his comrade, Ch'en Shao-pai, (1869–1934), were received at his home by Feng Ching-ju. In the same year, Feng Ching-ju organized and headed the Japan branch of the Resurgent China Association (Hsing-chung hui), the revolutionary party founded by Sun Yat-sen in 1894 in Honolulu. Feng Tzu-yu, at that time a boy of fourteen, joined the group as its youngest member. Thereafter, he remained one of Sun Yat-sen's trusted lieutenants until the latter's death in 1925. A party organizer and newspaper editor in Hong Kong, Vancouver, and San Francisco, Feng Tzu-yu contributed no less to the revolutionary cause than many of Sun Yat-sen's other followers who later occupied powerful positions in the Nationalist (Kuomintang) government, but Feng lost favor with Sun for his opposition to the policy of alliance with the Soviet Union. Somehow or another, he also failed to stage a comeback in the anti-Communist regime of Chiang Kai-shek. Having thus faded from the political scene, Feng Tzu-yu devoted the later part of his long life to writing copiously on the history of the anti-Manchu revolutionary movement of the pre-1912 period, which he knew intimately and in which he personally participated.

In his miscellaneous historical writings are to be found personal reminiscences of life at the Ta-t'ung School and of his early association with his fellow student, Su Man-shu. According to Feng, Man-shu was for two years in the regular class before he was promoted in the spring of 1900 to the honors section in which English was taught. By that time, Feng had already gone to Tokyo to enter the Ta-t'ung Advanced Institute founded by Liang Ch'i-ch'ao, and later to study at Waseda University. Years later,

Feng recalled that Man-shu was an indifferent student, even though the courses were not difficult, and he described Man-shu as being a rather dull, mediocre person. This account differs from that of another classmate who recently stated that Man-shu was among five or six students privileged to attend special evening classes in advanced Chinese taught by Liang Ch'i-ch'ao. It is possible that Man-shu was a slow starter, reflecting poor preparation at the Li-ch'i village school and desultory studies in Shanghai, but one who made excellent progress during the years at Ta-T'ung. On the other hand, Feng was impressed by Man-shu's talent for painting, which won the admiration of his schoolmates.

In 1902, while Lin Tzu-yüan was battling the crisis that had erupted at the Ta-t'ung School, he sent Man-shu to study in Tokyo together with Su Wei-han, an older cousin. Although they went to different schools, Man-shu taking the senior preparatory course at Waseda University, the cousins maintained close ties while in Tokyo. When Man-shu left for China the next year, Wei-han was one of very few friends who went to see him off.

CHAPTER 2

A Young Revolutionist Turned Buddhist

IN the first decade of the twentieth century, anti-Manchu agitation reached a climax in China. The seeds of revolution, first sown in the previous century, grew everywhere in the native soil; they began to sprout as well in foreign lands where overseas Chinese communities were to be found. Young students who had imbibed radical socio-political ideas at home and abroad constituted the vanguard of the revolution. Undaunted by repeated failures, and led by Sun Yat-sen, these young men were determined at all costs to restore the country to native rule. Contact with Japan and the West inspired in them a new national spirit, different from the fierce but blind patriotism that incited the Boxers into violent action. To build a stronger political following, the new leaders established their headquarters in foreign countries or in foreign-controlled cities which sheltered them from the persecution of the Manchu government. Thus, Chinese revolutionary activities in the early years of the twentieth century can be told briefly in a tale of three cities: Tokyo, Shanghai, and Hong Kong. Man-shu made a brief sojourn in each of them; in all of them he found himself in the rank and file of the revolutionary forces.

Su Man-shu began his apprenticeship as a fledgling revolutionary in the Chinese student community in Tokyo. Whereas only a handful of Chinese students were in Japan in 1895, their numbers swelled until as many as thirteen thousand may have been there in 1906. The largest group came from Kwantung, Man-shu's native province; many others came from the Yangtze valley provinces of Hunan, Hupei, Kiangsu, and Chekiang. They went to Japan to seek a modern education and often became fervent revolutionaries. Though of varied backgrounds and temperament, they shared a common aspiration to liberate China from the Manchu yoke, and some were resolved to transform traditional social and political institutions, once the Manchu dynasty was overthrown. Widely divergent political views were given expression by the Chinese student community, but those imbued with strong revolutionary ideals constituted the most colorful, articulate, and aggressive group. They were young and enthusiastic, bold in words and deeds. Political parties and associations were organized to promote their beliefs and to provide a focal point for their activities. Not a few students were endowed with literary talent as well as revolutionary zeal, and periodicals were founded to give voice to their views. It was with the radicals that Man-shu associated during his student days in Tokyo.

One young firebrand was Ch'in Li-shan, a Hunanese who had once studied at the Current Affairs Institute (Shih-wu hsüeh-t'ang) in Ch'ang-sha under the tutelage of Liang Ch'i-ch'ao and T'ang Ts'ai-ch'ang, both followers of K'ang Yu-wei. Later, in response to a summons from Liang, Ch'in Li-shan traveled to Tokyo to study at the Ta-t'ung Advanced Institute, where he became Feng Tzu-yu's schoolmate. In 1900, at the time of the Boxer uprising, Ch'in Li-shan left for Tientsin to urge the Boxer leaders to abandon their plans to annihilate foreign residents and to adopt a program of revolution against the Manchu regime. He failed in this mission and was thrown out by the Boxers as a "second-generation foreigner." He next went to Hankow to join T'ang Ts'ai-ch'ang, who was then organizing an Independent Army of the Yangtze regions to seize power in Central China. Upon the failure of the uprising and the death of T'ang and several of his followers, including some Ta-t'ung schoolmates, Ch'in Li-shan, who was then in Anhwei to incite a mutiny by naval personnel, fled to Japan. There he became a staunch member of the revolutionary camp; he withdrew his support of constitutional monarchy as advocated by K'ang Ya-wei in favor of the revolutionary policies of Sun Yat-sen. Thus, he sought to organize a meeting of Chinese students to mark the 242nd anniversary of China's conquest by the Manchus.

Perhaps the most colorful figure in this group was Chang Ping-lin (1868–1936), better known as Chang T'ai-yen, who became a close friend of Su Man-shu in later years. Today Chang's fame as a classical scholar overshadows his early revolutionary activities. Chang was a member of the "Congress" (Kuo-hui) convened at Chang Gardens in Shanghai under the sponsorship of T'ang Ts'ai-ch'ang. However, he opposed the monarchial intentions of the T'ang group. When his advice went unheeded, he cut off his queue as a token of defiance against the Manchu regime. After T'ang's abortive coup in Hankow, Chang accepted a position to teach Chinese at Soochow University, a school run by American missionaries. There, the political activist continued his outspoken advocacy of the revolutionary cause, reports of which soon reached government officials in Nanking. Fearing arrest, he left for Japan in early 1902. Shortly after his arrival, he went with Ch'in Li-shan to call upon Sun Yat-sen in Yokohama. His autobiography relates that he was well received by Sun and walked with him to the Hall of Central Harmony to the accompaniment of martial music. More than one hundred of Sun's followers assembled for a feast given in his honor, and the event sealed the bond of friendship between these two men.

Sometime in April 1902, Chang Ping-lin conceived the idea of holding the afore-mentioned student meeting to arouse and reinforce patriotic sentiments among the Chinese in Japan. Chang himself drafted the manifesto in an elegant classical idiom. In one passage, after having referred to the massacre of the Chinese people and the devastation of Chinese cities during the Manchu conquest, he wrote: "ceremonial robes and caps henceforth became the degrading queues and braided hair; when consulted by the emperor, ministers who used to sit were now required to kneel. Once these dogs and shaggy beasts were well situated in comfortable quarters, pitiable indeed was the lot of the Chinese people, good enough only to be slaves and menials! Living in constant fear of flogging and whipping, how could they participate in government affairs? As for the officials, without even the ability to suppress petty larcenists, how could they be expected to resist and fight Caucasians? How absurd!"[1] The manifesto was well received by the Chinese student population in Tokyo, and several hundred students planned to attend the meeting, but it was suppressed by the Japanese police at the request of the Chinese envoy to Japan. Only a handful of Sun Yat-sen's comrades observed the occasion in a Yokohama restaurant.

The spirit of the young revolutionaries, nevertheless, was undaunted. To weld themselves together in a common cause, in the winter of 1902 they founded the Youth Association (Ch'ing-nien hui). Apparently inspired by Mazzini's La Giovine Italia (Young Italy), but in order not to attract undue public attention, they chose a seemingly innocuous name for their organization rather than the more conspicuous Young China as was first suggested. Among its founding members, most of them students from Waseda, were Yeh Lan, Ch'in Yü-liu, Chang Chi, Feng Tzu-yu, and Su Man-shu. Ch'en Tu-hsiu, later one of the original founders of the Chinese Communist party, was a member of the organization and friend of Su Man-shu and his companions.

Chiefly instrumental in the establishment of the Youth Association were Yeh Lan and Ch'in Yü-liu (1879–1937), both natives of Kiangsu. Ch'in also drafted the association's regulations. Both young men were active in Chinese student affairs, but they soon left for Shanghai. Thereafter, little is heard of Yeh Lan except for a period of brief association with the *National People's Daily*, a newspaper with which Man-shu was also connected. On the other hand, upon his return to China, Ch'in Yü-liu busily engaged himself in education and political activities. As a political activist, he participated in the Ch'ang-sha incident of 1904, the 1911 Revolution, the anti-Yüan Shih-k'ai campaign of 1913, in which he was arrested and imprisoned for several years, and the 1927 Northern Expedition. On most of these occasions, he operated from his native city of Wu-hsi, where he was four times a magistrate. Though a veteran revolutionary, Ch'in Yü-liu attained neither fame nor high position in his thirty-five years of active political life.

Among the members of the Youth Association, probably the best known figure was Chang Chi (1882–1947), who became in later years a conservative leader of the Nationalist party. As a member of the government, he served for several years (1928–32) as vice president and president of the Judicial *Yüan*. Chang Chi went to Japan in 1899 to study political science and economics at Waseda University, where his association with Ch'in Yü-liu and others resulted in his joining the Youth Association. Soon afterward, he was expelled from Japan as the ringleader of a group of Chinese students who had invaded the residence of a Chinese diplomat, the supervisor of Chinese military students in Japan, and forcibly cut off his queue, which they hung on the ceiling joist of a Chinese student clubhouse. Once he returned to Shanghai, Chang Chi was immediately recruited to work for the *Su-pao*, a periodical which Chang Ping-lin, who had earlier returned to China, was then editing.

Like other Chinese students at Waseda University, Su Man-shu was swept into the revolutionary vortex. He joined the Youth Association and made friends with a group of young people with similar aspirations. Thus, by the beginning of 1903, Man-shu already espoused revolutionary causes. Soon afterward, a desire to serve his country impelled him to study military science at Ch'eng-ch'eng Academy (Seizo Gakko), a preparatory school for future officers of the Japanese army. There he first met Liu San who was to become one of his closest friends. The son of a prosperous landowning family from the Shanghai countryside, Liu, like Man-shu, developed revolutionary sympathies as a student. In later years he continued his association with the revolutionary movement, but chose to operate behind the scenes and render quietly whatever help and service he could. He is known principally, however, as the recipient of most of the personal letters written by Man-shu which have been preserved.

As a student of military science and a young man imbued with strong nationalistic feelings, Su Man-shu became an active member of the Chinese Students' Anti-Russian Volunteer Corps when that organization was founded in April, 1903. Alarmed by Russia's designs upon Chinese territory and its armed occupation of Manchuria, Chinese students in Japan organized protest movements against Russian aggression. Their first acts were to found the Volunteer Corps, later called the Chinese Student Army, to volunteer for military training, and to call for war with Russia. More than five hundred Chinese students attended a meeting called by Yeh Lan, Ch'in Yü-liu, and Niu Yung-chien—later a military leader of the Kuomintang party. About one hundred and twenty students signed up for the corps, while another forty volunteered to work at the corps headquarters. Headed by a Chinese student in the Japanese Army Officer School, the Volunteer Corps was divided into three companies, each consisting of four platoons of ten students each. Su Man-shu was assigned to the fourth platoon of Company A. Yeh Lan, Ch'in Yü-liu and Niu Yung-chien, a platoon leader, were in Company B, as was Huang Hsing (1874–1916), who later became one of Sun Yat-sen's top deputies in the revolutionary struggle. Twelve female students joined the corps as nurses' aides.

Less than ten days after its formation, the corps was suppressed by the Japanese government at the request of Chinese diplomatic officials, who saw it as a façade for antigovernment revolutionary activities. Undaunted, such corps leaders as Yeh Lan and Ch'in Yü-liu went underground to form a new organization, the Association for the People's Military Education. Membership in the association was kept secret, but it is known that Su Man-shu and

Huang Hsing were members of the organization. The prospectus of the association, as drafted by Ch'in Yü-liu, indicated clearly that it was a militant group that advocated the overthrow of the Manchu government. In unequivocal terms, it stated: "Alas! the fate of our Volunteer Corps! Ever since its organization, how badly we have been mauled and humiliated! Crouching before the officials, we watched abjectly their every breath and endured patiently their foaming and spitting! Do we desire to work for the independence of our nation, or do we endeavor merely to protect the personal interests of the Manchu rulers? Clearly this needs no discussion. All our countrymen will agree with us in saying that the Manchus have murdered our forefathers and robbed us of our inheritance for over two hundred years. Even now they persecute our people and hand our land over to the foreigners, thus leading us to impending doom and national annihilation. The Manchus are our inveterate enemies!"[2] For maximum security reasons, membership in the association was limited to a small group of intimate friends. No place or date was set for its meetings. For this reason, it was able to survive until it merged in 1905 with the grand revolutionary alliance forged by Sun Yat-sen.

To implement the triple revolutionary strategies of propaganda, insurrection, and assassination, members of the association one after another departed for home to start revolutionary movements in their native districts. Huang Hsing returned to Ch'ang-sha; Ch'in Yü-liu went first to Shanghai and thence to Ch'ang-sha at Huang Hsing's invitation. Following in their footsteps a few months later, Su Man-shu sailed from Japan in September, 1903, on his way to Hong Kong via Shanghai.

It has been suggested that Man-shu was forced to leave Japan because of financial difficulties. If his revolutionary spirits were high, he was low in cash as he had always been. As a student in metropolitan Tokyo, he appears to have led a somewhat circumscribed existence. During his first year there, he lived in a cheap rooming house, ate coarse rice, and, to save expenses, kept his room unlighted at night. When questioned about this, he answered: "Since I have already done my lessons during the day, why should I bother to light a lamp?" There are two theories as to how he maintained himself financially at Ch'eng-ch'eng Academy; both involve his relationship with Wang Ta-hsieh, a diplomat who was then superintendent of Chinese students in Japan. Either Wang gave Man-shu a government scholarship, or, as a relative of the family, he himself provided the money for Man-shu's schooling. At the same time, Man-shu must have received support from Lin Tzu-yüan, but it was now cut off to force his withdrawal from revolutionary activities, news of which must have alarmed Lin as well as his relatives in Yokohama and Hsiang-shan. The government scholarship, if in fact he was ever awarded one, must also have been suspended in view of his connections with the Volunteer Corps. The main reason for his departure from Japan, however, was his desire as a member of the Association for the People's Military Education to become actively engaged in revolutionary activities in his native land. It was for this purpose that he armed himself with, among other things, a letter of introduction from Feng Tzu-yu to Ch'en Shao-pai, who had by that time settled in Hong Kong as the publisher of *The China Daily* (*Chung-kuo jih-pao*), an official organ of Sun Yat-sen's revolutionary party.

Su Man-shu's personal feelings as he departed from Japan are revealed in two poems he addressed to a friend and teacher:

Bidding Farewell to T'ang Kuo-tun
with two Poems and a Painting[3]

I

Rather than hail Ch'in as Emperor, Lu Lien drowned himself in the sea,
His floating body shrouded by a vast expanse of water and mist.
Our people are sadly forlorn and resentful; the hero too sheds his tears
On the mermaid's silk, which he sends as a gift to his friend.

II

Where the sea merges with the sky, dragons fight, their blood dark and gory.
With dishevelled hair I sing loudly, looking toward the great bounds of space.
The waters of the Yi sobbed and sobbed when the hero departed,
And the sky was aglow in the bright moonlight, as white as frost.

Both poems celebrate the spirit of self-sacrifice. In the first, the young poet fondly recalls the actions of the patriot Lu Lien, and in the second Man-shu compares himself to the ancient hero Ching K'o, who is pictured about to take leave of his friends on the banks of the river Yi and set out on his mission to assassinate the king of

Ch'in. The rulers of the Manchu dynasty are by implication as ruthless and authoritarian as the founder of the ancient Ch'in empire. The poet sees himself as an avenger of the suffering population.

While on shipboard between Japan and Shanghai, Man-shu addressed a suicide note to Lin Tzu-yüan, informing the latter of his intention to drown himself in the China Sea. The intended purpose of this act is unknown. It could be construed as a device to prevent the implication of his family in Hsiang-shan in the anti-Manchu activities that he was about to undertake. This interpretation of his motives would appear to conform with the events that transpired in the next two years.

Man-shu's apparent destination was Hong Kong, but he made a stopover at Shanghai to visit friends who had preceded him. Before his arrival in Shanghai in September, 1903, the arrest of two revolutionary writers had shaken the local Chinese intellectual community. The Chinese Educational Association (Chung-kuo chiao-yü hsüeh-hui) was founded in the fall of 1902 by Huang Tsung-yang, Ts'ai Yüan-pei, Chang Ping-lin, and Wu Ching-heng, all of whom were later to become influential in educational and intellectual circles. Shortly thereafter, some two hundred students withdrew from Nan-yang Public School to protest the suppression by school authorities of the freedom of political discussion. Joined by other students, among them Chang Shih-chao, from the Nanking Military Academy, and with the help of the Chinese Educational Association, they formed a new school called the Patriotic Student Society (Ai-kuo hsüeh-shê), which soon became a center of revolutionary activities. In the meantime, Chang Ping-lin, Chang Shih-chao, Wu Ching-heng, and others assumed the editorship of the *Su-pao*, which became a vehicle for the dissemination of antigovernment propaganda. They were joined in this effort by Chang Chi and Tsou Yung, who had just been deported from Japan for the queue-cutting escapade described earlier. After their arrival in Shanghai, the latter set forth his ideas on revolution in *The Revolutionary Army*, an inflammatory pamphlet for which Chang Ping-lin supplied a preface. This call for revolt was published in the *Su-pao*, along with several other articles of a similar, seditious nature.

The upsurge of agitation for revolution by young students and writers removed from government control in the International Settlement so alarmed government officials in Nanking, that the

British authorities were requested to arrest the *Su-pao* editors and remand them to Chinese custody. The British responded by ordering the arrest of Tsou, Chang, and other leaders. When the police arrived, everyone but Chang Ping-lin had fled the premises. Later Chang sent a letter to Tsou Yung from prison, asking him to surrender himself, which he did. The Chinese government failed in its effort, however, to gain extradition of the two men and had to content itself with their imprisonment in Shanghai after a trial by the Mixed Court of the International Settlement. Tsou and Chang were sentenced to prison terms of two and three years, respectively. Tsou Yung took ill and died a martyr to the cause just a few months before he was scheduled for release. Chang Ping-lin passed three years of imprisonment reading Buddhist and classical literature.

The suppression of the *Su-pao* which followed this incident did not deter the revolutionaries from founding the *National People's Daily* (*Kuo-min jih-jih pao*) in August, 1903, under the editorship of Chang Shih-chao and Chang Chi. Among its contributors was Ch'en Tu-hsiu, a former member like Chang Chi of the Youth Association in Tokyo. Another former member of the association, Su Man-shu, became affiliated with the *Daily* shortly thereafter. Immediately upon his arrival on the scene in October there appeared in rapid succession in the *National People's Daily* the two poems cited above, two articles entitled "Emma Goldman, the Heroine" and "Alas! We Cantonese!" and a partial translation of the first section of Victor Hugo's *Les Misérables.* These writings reveal a crude style and a passionate diction, reflecting both the immaturity of the writer (he was barely twenty at the time) and the strong sentiments which motivated him.

The article on Emma Goldman is a grandiloquent account of the words and deeds of the American anarchist and a glorification of the anarchist's role as an assassin. It reports the murder of President William McKinley in September, 1901, at the Pan-American Exposition in Buffalo, New York. According to the author, the assassin, Leon Czologosz, shot the president because he had been incited to action by Goldman's speeches. Her arrest and imprisonment are noted, and the Chinese reader is informed that, from behind bars, with the flag at half staff, she remarked: "The death of a president! What is so important about that? Every man is doomed to die, whether a noble prince or a poor laborer. Why should people condole and mourn the death of McKinley? Is it just because he happened to be a president? For my part, I would rather commiserate the death of a poor miserable fellow in the marketplace" (*MSCC*, I, 153–54).[4] Earlier, in reference to herself, she is reported to have said: "I am an anarchist and socialist. Anarchism aims to destroy the evil structure of present-day society and to educate the individual; it is not, however, a principle for physical violence" (*MSCC*, I, 153). Despite this assertion, the article lists recent assassination attempts by anarchists on the lives of European monarchs: Empress Elizabeth, the estranged wife of Emperor Francis Joseph of Austria-Hungary, who was killed in 1898 in Sweden; King Humbert of Italy in July, 1900; Emperor William II of Germany, who was wounded at the railway station in Bremen in March, 1901; and King Leopold II of Belgium in November, 1902. The article concludes: "Following this movement, one does not know how and where it's going to end!" (*MSCC*, I, 155).

The second article, a vitriolic attack on his fellow Cantonese, is also marked by an outpouring of strong emotions typical of the work of an agitated young man. Unlike the Goldman article which is couched in the literary style, this essay uses the vernacular idiom, one of very few examples of such usage prior to the vernacular language movement of a decade later. Its crudity of style may be said to result from its experimental nature rather than from any inability of the author to handle the Chinese language. Its immature content notwithstanding, Man-shu succeeded in conveying to his readers a sense of urgency through a ringing denunciation of unpatriotic feelings and behavior. The Cantonese in Hong Kong are accused of connivance with foreigners and of fawning servility to the British. Cantonese merchants in Yokohama and other Japanese cities are attacked for relinquishing their Chinese citizenship. "Alas!" he exclaims, "Whereas other people make their conquests through trade, we Chinese will lose our country on account of these merchants! Just imagine, what hope is there for our nation! How are we going to atone for the sins of the Cantonese? When I think of it, grief seizes me and tears of blood stain my sleeves. I can hardly continue to hold my brush!" (*MSCC*, I, 159).

Man-shu's work with the *National People's Daily* consisted mainly of translation into the Chinese vernacular of Victor Hugo's *Les Misérables*, which he entitled *Ts'an shê-hui* (The Miserable Society). Published serially from October 8 to December 1, 1903, the translation stopped in the middle of the eleventh chapter. A year later, it was brought out in book form by a Shanghai publisher as a joint work of Su Man-shu and Ch'en Tu-hsiu. The latter, who worked with Man-shu at the *National People's Daily*, was responsible for the revision and continuation of the translation, which came to fourteen chapters, still a mere fraction of the original work. The Chinese version is actually a patchwork in two parts: first, a free rendering, probably from English or Japanese considering his language skills at the time, of Book II, namely, "The Fall" in "Fantine" from the first section of Hugo's novel; second, an original story of approximately equal length, a sheer invention by Man-shu bearing little resemblance or relevance to the French novel.

The first part relates the story of the encounter of Charles Myriel, Bishop of D——, called Bishop Meng in the translation, and Jean Valjean, renamed Chin Hua-chien (Gold, China-humble). Faithfulness and accuracy were not a matter of concern to Man-shu, and he departed widely from the text in casting aspersions on the character of the good bishop and the motives of his action. Numerous changes were made in the text and whole sentences and paragraphs are omitted in the Chinese version; nevertheless, it reads rather smoothly, and the descriptive passages in this part distinguish it from the second, in which there is a greater reliance on the narrative art. Therein, Man-shu tells with a great deal of gusto his own story of the aspirations and adventures of a heroic figure, Ming Nan-tê (Enlightened Manly-virtue), a modern revolutionist endowed with the traits of a traditional Chinese *hsia*, the righteous hero who seeks to right wrongs in this world. As a short work of fiction inspired by *Les Misérables*, Man-shu's story is primarily an indictment of conventional society and authoritarian rule. It is an exposure of the treachery and ruthlessness of officialdom—the hypocrisy and abjectness of human nature. One episode describes the attempt by Nan-tê to assassinate Napoleon I in 1798. A member of a revolutionary faction, Nan-tê is disturbed by the monarchial intentions of Napoleon and seeks to destroy Napoleon before he is crowned emperor. With tongue in cheek, one of the characters in the novel states, "We French people are not to be compared to the abject Chinamen of the East, who regard their enemies who once murdered their forefathers as benevolent rulers and sage emperors" (*MSCC*, II, 243). Later, Nan-tê himself declares: "We French are a righteous and courageous people who, unlike the slavish Chinamen, will never submit to oppression and tyranny! How could we allow this damned President [Napoleon I] to become an absolute monarch and wield over us the power of life and death!" (*MSCC*, II, 254). Nan-tê plants a bomb along the route Napoleon takes to the theater, but it explodes seconds before the arrival of the presidential carriage. Nan-tê then shoots himself. This story of attempted assassination dramatizes in fictional form the ideas and aspirations of young Chinese revolutionaries of the time. The theme, to which Man-shu constantly reverted in his writings of this time, is in keeping with his personal sentiments and his previous activities in Japan.

For a short while, Su Man-shu taught at a school in Soochow. It cannot be ascertained whether he took this position before or after his work with the *National People's Daily*. Since Soochow was only several hours by train from Shanghai, it is also possible that he could have held the two jobs concurrently, both involving a minimum amount of formal attention. In any case, he did not remain long in either position. His tenure with the newspaper did not exceed the two-month period during which his *Misérable Society* was being published, while his connection with the Soochow school was perhaps only a matter of a few weeks. One thing however is certain; namely, Man-shu was not well paid in either position. Very likely, he volunteered to serve on the faculty in Soochow without compensation. His newspaper work was also primarily a labor of love. Most newspapers at that time enjoyed little financial backing, and this was especially true of the publications of revolutionary groups, which consisted mostly of men of deep political conviction but shallow purses. Thus, even though he was busily engaged in writing and teaching, he was just as penniless as he had been when a poor student in Japan.

The pressure of finances occasioned a dramatic exit from the Shanghai scene in early December. Man-shu was living at that time with Chang Shih-chao, Ch'en Tu-hsiu, and another friend, Ho Mei-shih. One day when Chang and Ch'en were out, Man-shu invited Ho Mei-shih to the theater, where, apparently following a well-conceived plan, he pretended that he had forgotten to take any money with him and left Ho at the theater while he returned to the house. Seizing thirty dollars that belonged to Chang Shih-chao, he left immediately for the docks and the first boat to Hong Kong. Having had the foresight to ask Feng Tzu-yu for a letter of introduction to Ch'en Shao-pai, the door to the headquarters of *The China Daily* was opened, and it was there that he took temporary lodging.

The China Daily had been founded by Sun Yat-sen in late 1899 as a party organ and placed under the management of Ch'en Shao-pai, Sun's closest personal friend. Two years later in 1901, *The China Daily* moved to new quarters in Yung-lo Street, Hong Kong. Sun Yat-sen stayed there for a week on his way from Japan to Hanoi, and at one time or another it provided temporary shelter for other revolutionaries, including Ch'in Li-shan and Niu Yung-chien. Feng Tzu-yu, who was later to succeed Ch'en Shao-pai in the editorship of the paper, was at the time its Tokyo correspondent and therefore in a position to recommend Man-shu as a comrade.

Obscurity veils Man-shu's activities in Hong Kong. He seems to have led a quiet, isolated existence. He did not make as many friends as he had done in Yokohama and Shanghai, nor did his relations with Ch'en Shao-pai and others in the newspaper office mature into friendship. The literary talent that he had demonstrated with the Shanghai paper was neglected, and he failed to publish in *The China Daily*. For unknown reasons, a mood of despondency seems to have settled upon him during this time. His revolutionary zeal was not given outlet, nor did any impulse to write bear fruit. He left Hong Kong for Kwangtung as unobtrusively as he had come. No one at *The China Daily* seemed to miss him when he disappeared. Several explanations have been offered for his decision to return to his native province. Now that he was so near his family home, homesickness may have prompted his return, or the pursuit of a secret project, such as the assassination of a Manchu official, may have motivated his trip to mainland Kwangtung. It appears that neither was the case, for his journey ended at an old, dilapidated temple in Hui-chou, southern Kwangtung. There he took the tonsure and entered the temple as a Buddhist novice. In our knowledge of his early life, there is no indication of any previous interest in religion, least of all Buddhism, nor of any influences in family background or education which might have prompted him to take monastic vows. The change from a wide-eyed young revolutionary to an alms-begging novice was drastic; the reason may have been the simple desire to escape an arranged marriage.[5]

Little glamor, such as he later pretended, surrounded his initiation into the Buddhist order. Instead of learning Buddhist scriptures in a large monastery from a well-known teacher of the law, Man-shu led a life of destitution in an old temple. In company with an old monk, he earned his daily fare begging for alms. The oppression of hunger and poverty rather than the "rigors of the monastic order" induced him to steal two small coins from the old monk, who had gone out begging for food, as well as the ordination certificate of another monk who had recently passed away. The certificate was used as a passport for his return trip to Hong Kong. One day in February, 1904, dressed in a Buddhist robe and sandals, he appeared again at the offices of *The China Daily* to the astonishment of his colleagues. By then he had assumed the Buddhist name Man-shu (from Manjusri, a Bodhisattva), by which he became known to his contemporaries and posterity.

His second stay in Hong Kong during February and March, 1904, was even briefer than the first. On March 13, he unexpectedly met a villager from Hsiang-shan, who returned to Li-ch'i with news of his activities. His father Chieh-sheng was seriously ill at that moment; the villager was immediately sent back to Hong Kong to ask Man-shu to return home. The young man refused. Two days later on March 15, Su Chieh-sheng died at the age of sixty; neither of his sons was at his side. Man-shu remained in Hong Kong and Hsü-t'ing was in Kobe, Japan, where he was engaged in business.

Somewhat earlier Man-shu had been frustrated in an attempt to assassinate K'ang Yu-wei. *The China Daily* was engaged in a bitter dispute with *The Commercial Journal*, an organ of K'ang Yu-wei's Reform party, edited by Hsü Chun-mien, Man-shu's former principal at the Ta-t'ung School. Severely critical of K'ang's support of the Manchu regime and his loyalty to the emperor, and fearing the growing influence of the reform party in Hong Kong, Man-shu threatened to kill K'ang Yu-wei with a gun, apparently forgetting for the moment the tenets of his new faith. He was deterred from carrying out his plot by Ch'en Shao-pai. In this connection, we may charitably surmise that his determination to sever all family ties, even though his father was seriously ill, may have been motivated by the fear of implicating his family and clan in his activities. And yet, the revolutionary ardor which he espoused had cooled since his return from the monastery. As he entered his twenty-first year, teaching and writing rather than politics were to occupy his attention, even though occasionally the smoldering spark of his revolutionary spirit would blaze up again.

CHAPTER 3

Man-shu and His Literary Circle

DURING Su Man-shu's early manhood, new ideas and influences deluged the Chinese literary world. Political agitation against the Manchu regime left its mark on the intellectual thinking and literary productions of the period. Regarding the late Ch'ing novelists' satirical thrusts against official corruption and social decadence as mild and ineffective, a new generation of writers advocated a literature that would serve as the vanguard of political revolution, the aim of which was to overthrow the Manchu dynasty and the two-thousand-year old monarchical system. These men not only rebelled against the domination of Chinese literature by conservative Confucian scholars loyal to the Manchu regime, but were similarly engaged in literary and political battles with erstwhile reformists such as K'ang Yu-wei and Liang Ch'i-ch'ao. In place of the latter, a group of new intellectuals arose, several of whom, notably Chang Ping-lin, Chang Shih-chao, and Ch'en Tu-hsiu, have already been encountered as acquaintances of Su Man-shu. Soon he was to widen his circle of friends to include other men of letters resident in Shanghai, such as the members of the Association for the Preservation of National Learning (Kuo-hsüeh pao-ts'un hui). Man-shu was also acquainted with Liu Shih-p'ei (1884–1919) and his wife Ho Chen, both pioneer Chinese anarchists who were later to become intelligence agents for the Manchu government. Maintaining contact with a wide circle of friends and acquaintances, and only occasionally troubled by their petty quarrels and activities, Su Man-shu personally led a quiet, untrammeled existence, thus earning himself the respect of all who knew him. If Man-shu stayed aloof from the political squabbles of his fellow intellectuals, emotionally he was susceptible to the vagaries and changing moods of a lonely young man. Family life and affection eluded him, and he sought to re-establish contact with Kawai, his Japanese "mother." In his twenty-fourth year, they met again—their reunion being one of the happiest occasions in his life.

Returning to Shanghai in March, 1904, Man-shu visited briefly with Yeh Lan at the office of the Society for National Learning (Kuo-hsüeh-shê), a publishing house founded by returned students from Japan for the translation and distribution of revolutionary materials. Then he proceeded from Shanghai on a long journey that took him to South and Southeast Asia, namely, Siam (Thailand), Ceylon, and possibly Annam (North Vietnam). Where he got the financial resources for this trip is not known, though there are several accounts of a windfall that befell him at that time. Perhaps the most likely explanation is that he came into some money after his father's death. According to one of his friends, it was transmitted to him by a younger brother of Huang-shih, Su Chieh-sheng's first wife. This is quite feasible, for although Man-shu never returned to the Su family at Hsiang-shan, he did maintain irregular contact with his kinsfolk in Kwangtung and Japan.

There is little information on his trip to South and Southeast Asia beyond his own statements, which are often compounded of poetry and fiction. It is said that he taught, presumably English, at the Young Men's Association in Bangkok, where he studied Sanskrit with a Buddhist master named Chiao-hsi-mo. He is also said to have resided for a time at the Bodhi Temple in Ceylon. Postscripts to his own paintings leave the impression that he was in Siam from 1903 to 1904, but a stay of such duration does not seem possible, considering the crowded events of his life during these two years. More likely, the trip lasted for only a few months from spring to fall in 1904. The visit to South Asia is important, however, for it was then that he drank directly at the fountainhead of Buddhism. Man-shu may have taken his priestly vows at a temple in Annam, branding his arm instead of his head as was done in China. One of his students, who studied with him shortly afterward in the winter of 1904, recalled that "the teacher once showed me a photograph of him, which was taken when he was receiving instruction in the temple in Annam. There he sat under a big tree, his right shoulder completely bare and the scar on his arm dimly visible."[1] But the most significant aspect of the trip was his introduction to Sanskrit, to which he was to devote himself a few years later. It opened up to him the new vista of classical Indian literature, which engrossed his attention as much as Buddhism itself ever did.

On his return to China, Man-shu occupied himself between late 1904 and September, 1906, with teaching, mainly English and occasionally painting. He got his first job at the Industrial School in Ch'ang-sha, Hunan, through the recommendation of Ch'in Yü-liu, the academic dean. At the invitation of Huang Hsing, Ch'in Yü-liu came to Ch'ang-sha from Shanghai, where he and Yeh Lan had founded the Society for National Learning. There he helped organize and lead the China Restoration Society (Hua-hsing hui), a revolutionary organ of young political activists similar in its aims to those organized by Chinese students in Tokyo. While in Ch'ang-sha, Ch'in also taught at two other schools, Ming-tê and Ching-cheng, with Huang Hsing and Chang Chi. Many of the students of these three men later became the bulwark of the revolutionary movement in Hunan. The China Restoration Society gained a membership of some four to five hundred persons, mostly drawn from education circles, and established a link with the Elder Brothers' Association (Kê-lao hui), one of the most powerful secret societies of the time. The date for an uprising against the government was set for the tenth day of the tenth month (November 16, 1904), the occasion of the seventieth birthday anniversary of the empress dowager. The assemblage of civil and military officials in Ch'ang-sha for the birthday celebration appeared to be a prime opportunity for revolt. But the news leaked out to the provincial government three weeks before the attempted coup, and many insurgents were arrested; Huang Hsing and Ch'in Yü-liu barely escaped with their lives.

Su Man-shu surprisingly remained at Ch'ang-sha after the abortive coup to continue undisturbed his teaching at the Industrial School. One would surmise that because of his association with Ch'in Yü-liu and Huang Hsing, he would have joined the revolutionaries and become implicated in the plot, but apparently this was not the case. It is necessary, therefore, to conclude that he was less interested than before in politics and revolution. A factor in dampening his previous revolutionary ardor almost certainly was Buddhist ideals and his priestly vows. Although Man-shu continued to associate with his activist friends and occasionally to give vent to patriotic outcries, he began to lose interest in politics and no longer participated in antigovernment activities. The change was so complete that posterity has usually failed to recognize the kind of revolutionary he was in his early youth.

Man-shu did not leave Ch'ang-sha until the summer of 1905, when he went to Shanghai to visit Ch'in Yü-liu, who had taken refuge there. The latter reports that Man-shu was well provided with funds and squandered them in the company of professional female entertainers known as "sing-song girls." The source of his income, other than that derived from teaching, is unknown. The same autumn he made his first trip to West Lake in Hangchow. Its scenic views and secluded Buddhist temples so attracted Man-shu that he was to visit it again and again in years to come. Although he headquartered in Shanghai and took many trips to Canton, Soochow, and Nanking, he visited Hangchow frequently because it provided a peaceful environment for contemplation and creative endeavors.

His state of mind at that time was best expressed in the following poem written during a sojourn at White Clouds Monastery on West Lake:

Amidst the dense white clouds which embrace Thunder Peak,
Stand a few wintry plum trees, their red blooms clothed with snow.
After a vegetable repast I sink slowly, completely into a deep meditation,
As the sound of a distant bell falls on shadows in the monastery pool.

Inspired by the scenic beauty of West Lake and environs, he painted a number of pictures, one of which he sent to Ch'en Tu-hsiu in Anhwei. Ts'ai Shou, a Cantonese friend, in an inscription to another painting, gave his first impression of the young poet-monk as follows:

> In the autumn of 1905 . . . as I one day passed by the cliff in front of Soul-Secluded Monastery, I saw a young man with a shaved head sitting precariously near the edge of the stone railing. Although he wore a Buddhist robe, he had inside it a woolen sweater that reached to his neck. His sad but imposing looks oppressed one who watched him. I figured that he must have been a remarkable fellow who had been forced into monkhood much against his will.
>
> Now, as I look at this picture, I realize that Man-shu too must have visited West Lake in the same year. So I ask him about it and discover that the monk I encountered that day was no other than Man-shu himself. (*MSCC*, IV, 26)

Man-shu went next to Nanking to take a teaching position with the Army Elementary School. There he renewed his friendship with Liu San and made the acquaintance of Chao Sheng (Chao Pai-hsien), a young colonel in the New Army recently organized by the government. Like many young army officers, Chao Sheng sympathized with the revolutionary cause, and, together with Huang Hsing, he was later to become the chief architect of the famous Yellow Flower Mound uprising at Canton on April 27, 1911. That insurrection crumbled when Chao Sheng failed to enter the city gate with reinforcements at the appointed time, leaving Huang Hsing to face the government troops with a small band of followers. Outnumbered, Huang Hsing fled, leaving behind him many dead comrades. Of these, seventy-two were later buried at Yellow Flower Mound, by which name this uprising came to be known. Grieved at his failure, Chao Sheng soon died, another martyr to the revolution.

In his *Random Notes from a Swallow's Mausoleum*, Man-shu has left the following account of his friendship with Chao Sheng:

> Chao Pai-hsien had the ambition of reforming the world and bringing peace to the country. When I taught at the Chiang-nan Army Elementary School, Pai-hsien was a colonel of the third regiment in the New Army. It was then that I came to know him and was impressed by his military talents. Everytime he came to visit me, he would send his soldiers over with a salted duck and a pot of rice wine. Pai-hsien was as brave in drinking as I was in eating. After getting intoxicated, he would sing loudly, his hand on his sword, below the wind-wafted willow twigs. Sometimes we would gallop our horses together along this city of coiling dragons and crouching tigers. These were indeed moments of great joy! (*MSCC*, II, 47)

Su Man-shu was stricken with sorrow when he heard of Chao Sheng's death. In March, 1912, he sent a painting entitled "Drinking the Horses in a Desolate City" to a friend in Canton to be burned at Chao Sheng's grave. "I promised Chao this picture when we stayed together in Nanking," he wrote to his friend. "Now I have the same intention as the ancient who hung up his sword after his friend's death. After this picture, I can hardly bear to draw another" (*MSCC*, I, 242). One should add here, as a matter of record, that the picture was spared its fate and Man-shu continued to paint for other friends. Early 1906 found Man-shu back in Ch'ang-sha, this time teaching painting at Ming-tê school. One of his students there was Ch'en Kuo-fu, who later became an important member of the Nationalist party. Soon Man-shu left for Wu-hu, Anhwei, to take a position at Wan-chiang School. Among the faculty were Ch'en Tu-hsiu, Chang Shih-chao, and Liu Shih-p'ei, all friends of his.

Though still a young man of twenty-three, the same age as Man-shu, Liu Shih-p'ei had already published widely in the field of Chinese classical studies, as well as political writings of a polemic nature. In 1903, Chang Ping-lin and Ts'ai Yüan-p'ei encouraged him to work for the revolutionary cause as a newspaper writer and editor. Man-shu may have met Liu at that time, but their friendship did not develop until after they were together at Wan-chiang. It was on a trip they took together from Wu-hu to Shanghai that Liu Shih-p'ei first introduced Man-shu to Liu Ya-tzu.

During the summer vacation of 1906, Man-shu and Ch'en Tu-hsiu left Wu-hu for a trip to Japan, which he had not visited since 1903. This time he made an attempt to find Kawai, whose memory must have lingered fondly but vaguely in his mind for years. He undertook the journey with some expectation and suffered disappointment when he failed to see Kawai that summer. Kawai herself confirmed this event in a "Preface to Man-shu's Painting Album," which was published the following year (1907):

> In his childhood my son was by no means intelligent; moreover, he was often sick. He was odd by nature, but loved painting and traveling. Since he left home in the early years,[2] we had not seen each other for a decade and more. In a twinkling of the eye, he is now already twenty-four. Last summer, dressed in his Buddhist garb, he came east to pay me a visit. Unfortunately, I happened to be in the countryside and we missed each other. (*MSCC*, IV, 16–17)

As this piece is expressed in good literary Japanese, the question has been raised of its actual authorship. But even if someone, perhaps Man-shu himself, wrote it for Kawai, the fact of their long separation and Man-shu's attempt to locate her in 1906 is indisputable.

When Man-shu returned to Wu-hu in August of the same year, he found the school in a chaotic condition—"so utterly strange as to be incredible," as he described it in a letter to Liu San. Consequently, two weeks after the mid-autumn festival he quit his job and left for Shanghai with two other teachers. Once there, he immediately went on a short trip to Hangchow, where he "feasted his eyes in silent joy" as he sailed on West Lake. But this kind of idyllic existence did not last long, for he had to face the practical problem of making a living. Back in Shanghai, he found himself adrift and without money; he could not even afford a haircut or a bath, his purse having been empty since his departure from Wu-hu. In vain he waited for a letter from Lin Tzu-yüan, his cousin in Japan; lacking the courage to seek assistance from his relatives in Hsiang-shan, he was stranded in that great metropolis. Some of his letters requesting financial assistance, such as the ones with which he bombarded Liu San, must have produced some effect. With occasional help from friends, Man-shu managed to live on in Shanghai, taking up temporary lodgings in the secret headquarters of the Shanghai branch of the China Alliance (Chung-kuo t'ung-meng hui). This grand alliance of Chinese revolutionary parties had been forged on August 20, 1905, in Tokyo by Sun Yat-sen, Huang Hsing, Chang Chi (the latter two men had fled to Japan after the failure of the Ch'ang-sha insurrection), Wang Chao-ming, Hu Han-min, Sung Chiao-jen, Feng Tzu-yu, Ma Chün-wu, and many others. Even though Man-shu had withdrawn from all political activity by that time, he still maintained friendly relations with the revolutionaries; thus, he was well received by them and was given free lodgings in their Shanghai headquarters.

On the Chinese New Year (February 13, 1907), Man-shu again traveled to Japan, accompanied this time by Liu Shih-p'ei and his wife, Ho Chen. It was then that a reunion with Kawai, a white-haired woman of almost sixty, was finally effected. Mother and son met in a restaurant at Omori, a town near Kamata, between Tokyo and Yokohama. The meeting took place in the summer of 1907, according to an eyewitness who also served as an interpreter.[3] It was a quiet, tearful occasion. In a second meeting a few days later, Kawai introduced Man-shu to her Japanese husband, an old man of good family. At this time, Kawai gave him three photographs: one of himself about two or three years old, dressed in a Japanese costume and sitting on Kawai's lap; a second, probably taken on the same occasion, shows him standing between an elderly Japanese couple, his maternal grandparents; a third was of his elder sister by Kawai's first Japanese husband. Apropos of these pictures, which he sent to Liu San in early August, 1907, Man-shu wrote: "My grandparents died several years ago, and now only the three of us, my mother, my elder sister, and myself are living in this world, inseparable from each other as body from shadow." In this letter as in others, Man-shu made no mention of Kawai's second Japanese husband with whom she was living.[4] Even though Man-shu may have taken kindly to Kawai's remarriage, he did try to hide it from his friends, none of whom knew or even suspected it. This also made it necessary for him to live with friends rather than with Kawai during his sojourn in Japan, even though he frequently visited her and accompanied her on trips to the seashore.

For several months, Man-shu stayed with Chang Ping-lin at the Tokyo office of the *People's Report (Min-pao)*, before moving to the quarters of the *Tien Yee News (T'ien-i pao)*, a newspaper founded by Liu Shih-p'ei and Ho Chen. The *People's Report*, a monthly first published in October, 1905, was the official organ of the China Alliance. According to a statement in its April, 1906 issue (Volume 3), the principal goals of the *People's Report* were cited in rather quaint English to be:

1. The destruction of the present autocratic Dynasty;
2. The establishment of republic Government;
3. The equal enjoyment of land for all people;
4. Universal peace by brotherhood of human kind.

Among its leading writers were Hu Han-min, Wang Chao-ming (Wang Ching-wei), Sung Chiao-jen, and Chang Chi, all important members of the China Alliance and later of the Nationalist party. Released from jail in Shanghai in June, 1906, Chang Ping-lin went directly to Tokyo, there to receive a hero's welcome from the revolutionaries. He joined the China Alliance and succeeded Chang Chi as editor of the *People's Report*. According to Chang Ping-lin himself, the journal was so popular among Chinese students resident in Japan that upon its first anniversary in October, 1906, thousands of people joined in the celebration. The paper also found its way to China where it was read surreptitiously and with great fervor by the student population. In November, 1908, after three years of publication, the *People's Report* was banned by the Japanese government. Two years later it was revived for two months in Paris, though it is believed that the later issues were also actually published in Japan.

The *Tien Yee News* (June, 1907–March, 1908), primarily a private enterprise of Liu Shih-p'ei and his wife, was the first Chinese publication to advocate anarchism and socialism. Its stated aims, as stipulated in English in the November 30, 1907, issue (Vols. 11–12), were as follows:

1. To realize internationalism, abolishing all the national and social distinctions;
2. To revolt against all authorities of the world;
3. To overthrow all the political systems of the present time;
4. To realize communism;
5. To realize absolute equality of man and Asian woman.

The last objective, fervently advocated by Ho Chen, was a pointed reference to the fact that while men and women were legally equal in some Western countries, no such equality existed between the two sexes in Asia. The *Tien Yee News* also promoted communism in addition to anarchism, publishing in the spring of 1908 the first Chinese version of the *Communist Manifesto* of Marx and Engels.

For Man-shu, the year 1907 was one of great creativity and important scholarly endeavors. He did not join the China Alliance as Liu Shih-p'ei and Ho Chen had done after their arrival in Japan, but he did contribute a number of articles, miscellaneous notes, translations, and paintings to both journals. He also devoted himself in the first five months in Tokyo to the study of the Sanskrit language and Buddhist literature. These subjects so fascinated him that he planned enthusiastically for a trip to India with Chang Ping-lin, but he was never able to carry his plans to fruition because of a lack of financial support. He did, however, begin the compilation of an eight-volume (*chüan*) *Sanskrit Grammar* (*Fan-wen tien*). According to the author's preface, the idea was born three years before at the suggestion of "Chiao-hsi-mo," the Siamese Buddhist monk with whom he had studied Sanskrit. By that time, the master had already passed away, and it was to fulfill a devout wish that Man-shu undertook the work. It too would meet a long-felt demand, since there was no Chinese work on the subject. First projected as a four-volume work to be entitled *Elementary Sanskrit Grammar*, it was expanded later into the announced eight-volume work.

Man-shu's *Sanskrit Grammar* was based on the English works of Friedrich Max Müller (*A Sanskrit Grammar for Beginners*, 1866) and Monier Monier-Williams (*An Elementary Grammar of the Sanskrit Language*, 1846; *A Practical Grammar of the Sanskrit Language*, 1857). To these Man-shu added material from available T'ang and Sung dynasty native sources. The publication of the first volume was advertised in the fifteenth issue of the *People's Report* (summer, 1907) and the sixth issue of the *Tien Yee News*

(September, 1907). Man-shu also sent announcements of the forthcoming publication to his friends in China. From the table of contents of the first volume, which appeared in advertisements in the two periodicals, we know that the book contained, besides the prefaces and poetic inscriptions to be mentioned later, a general survey (*viniscaya*) of the Sanskrit language, the alphabet, a chart of Chinese and Roman transcription, an interpretation of the alphabet in the sutras, vowels (*mātrkā*), special vowels, nasalization symbols (*anusvāra*), final aspirate symbols (*visarga*), consonants (*vyañjana*), vowel changes (*guna* and *vrddhi*), half vowel, five classes of articulation, vowel *sandhi*, consonant *sandhi*, numerals, consonant clusters and so forth. One of the appendices consisted of the *Heart Sutra* (*Prajnāpāramitāhrdaya*) in original Sanskrit, with both Chinese and English translation, the latter by F. Max Müller. While Man-shu undoubtedly completed the first volume, it cannot be ascertained what stage the other seven volumes reached, if they were ever actually completed. Unfortunately, the cost of printing the book in Japan in three foreign languages (Chinese, Sanskrit, and English) was high, and the whole project had to be abandoned—a great loss to the world of Sino-Sanskrit scholarship.

Man-shu was encouraged in the writing and publication of the *Sanskrit Grammar* by Chang Ping-lin, with whom he began to be closely associated at that time. A prodigious scholar, Chang was himself deeply engrossed in Buddhism and was well learned in its lore as a result of three years of intensive study in prison. Once he even thought of becoming a Buddhist monk himself. A preface which he wrote for Man-shu is preserved in two different versions: one for the *Elementary Sanskrit Grammar*; the other for the revised and expanded work. Both prefaces, which vary only slightly in content, provide a running account of Chinese translations of Buddhist literature, emphasizing the importance of grammar in learning and translating from Sanskrit texts. Then, in the role of an older and more mature scholar, Chang addressed his young friend as follows: "Since the monk Man-shu knows the Sanskrit language, he should further its study with the aim of translating the doctrines of the Buddhist masters to supplement the existing works of the Mahayana. Would that he could exert himself in this effort and not content himself with pursuing vainly and noisily a fleeting name!" (*MSCC*, IV, 14–15). This last sentence was deleted from the second version.

Contributions by other friends included a preface by Liu Shih-p'ei, a Buddhist hymn by Ho Chen, and a poem by Ch'en Tu-hsiu. Of these, the most important is Liu Shih-p'ei's preface, in which he left little doubt that Man-shu did complete the book, praising it as a work of substantial practical value for the study of Buddhist literature and as a key with which to unlock the mysterious meaning of Sanskrit works and names. To confirm Man-shu in his intention to take the westward journey to India, Liu devoted the major part of his preface to a survey of linguistic and literary relationships between China and India, listing the beneficial influences of Sanskrit on the Chinese language, rhetoric, and logic.

At the same time, Man-shu's other publication effort, a volume of his paintings, proved to be equally futile. While engaged in his Sanskrit studies, Man-shu executed also a number of paintings, mostly at his friends' request. Even as early as his Ta-t'ung period, Man-shu had impressed his schoolmates by his talent for painting. In later years, as his artistic ability and fame grew, such was the admiration and demand for his painting—his landscapes on Chinese-style folded fans proved to be most popular—that he once said jokingly that he would ask in exchange for each of his paintings a photo of his admirer if it was a woman, but would reject all requests from men—a threat which, luckily, he failed to carry out. Such a collection of his pictures already existed in 1907, and Ho Chen, his student in painting, decided to have them published in an album. Again a lack of funds wrecked the project. However, many of his pictures did appear in the art and literary supplements of the *People's Report* and in the *Tien Yee News*. In the fifth issue of the latter publication were also published four documents relating to Man-shu's album, which included prefaces by Kawai, Chang Ping-lin and Man-shu, and a postscript by Ho Chen herself.

Kawai's preface, referred to earlier, states that after the first disappointment, Man-shu's reunion with her finally took place in the summer of 1907, the same summer in which the preface was written.[5] It refers likewise to Man-shu's plan to visit India to study Sanskrit. To reinforce his resolve, Kawai introduced the preface with the following poem (in Chinese):

The moon having departed from mid-sky, the clouds give chase to the wind,
As a wild goose casts its lonely shadow, desolately, on the setting sun.
(This scene is found frequently in my son's pictures)

I would look for your homeward letters from across the Eastern Sea—
My son, how many cliffs of the Holy Mountain have you reached?
(One of the pictures my son painted is entitled
"Shaking my Buddhist Cassock on the Holy Mountain")

Since there was so much talk about this grand journey, his failure to bring it off must have been another disappointment in his life.

Among Man-shu's miscellaneous writings of this period are two short pieces commemorating the recent death of two heroines: Clemence Louise Michel (1830–1905), a French anarchist, called *la Vierge rouge de Montmarte*; and Ch'iu Chin (1875–1907), a Chinese revolutionary martyr, known as the Lady Knight-Errant of the Mirror Lake (*Chien-hu nü-hsia*). Similarly dedicated to the cause of revolution, the two women differ in a number of respects. While Louise Michel was the illegitimate child of a servingmaid and a young noble, Ch'iu Chin came from a respectable gentry-scholar family; she was, however, separated from her husband because of incompatibility. An anarchist propagandist and a member of the Communards, Michel was first exiled as a convict and later condemned to a long imprisonment. On the other hand, Ch'iu Chin, a member of the Triad Society (a secret society also known as the Society of Heaven and Earth) and the China Alliance, was summarily executed without a trial when she was caught in an insurrection plot in Chekiang. Both women were school teachers but the Chinese had the added distinction of being also a poet. It was to a volume of her poetic remains collected by Chang Ping-lin shortly after Ch'iu Chin's death (in July, 1907) that Man-shu contributed a preface, extolling her for "facing death bravely as if returning home." In his eulogy of Michel, Man-shu quoted from an inscription on a portrait of hers in his possession: "Louise Michel was really a kind-hearted woman, who dreamed of bettering humanity. Personally she would not have harmed a fly." Then he added: "Alas! Alas! As I stretch my gaze toward this dusty world, all the living creatures there are lost in pain and suffering. Who would rise again to guide them like Michel, the master helmsman?"

Since his reunion with Kawa, Man-shu had been shuttling back and forth between Japan and China. Unfortunately, during a trip to Shanghai in the same year he was plagued by sickness and destitution, chronic troubles that pursued him in later years. As Kawai herself reported, Man-shu suffered from constant illnesses in his childhood; they recurred and worsened at a time when he should have been in the prime of his life. In September, 1907, on his way from Tokyo to Shanghai, he was laid up in bed for eight days with a severe cold at an inn in Nagasaki. What little financial resources he had been able to obtain from his elder sister, Kawai's daughter, and friends were quickly dissipated by medical and hotel bills. Thus, he had barely set foot in Shanghai when he had to devise ways and means of raising funds for a return trip to Japan.

While in Shanghai, Man-shu stayed with Huang Chieh (Huang Hui-wen) and Teng Shih (Teng Ch'iu-mei)—at one time he was so hard up that Huang Chieh had to lend him a dollar for pocket money—at the library of the Association for the Preservation of National Learning. The association was founded in 1905 by a group of Cantonese intellectuals in Shanghai, headed by Teng and Huang. Under the façade of a scholarly name, it aimed to arouse popular revolutionary sentiment through the dissemination of the writings of Ming dynasty patriots who had refused to serve the Manchu regime. The main activity of the association was the publication of the *Journal on Chinese Learning* (*Kuo-ts'ui hsüeh-pao*), which appeared monthly in eighty-two issues from 1905 to 1911, in which year it ceased publication after the success of the revolution. Besides Teng Shih and Huang Chieh, the chief editors of the *Journal*, Chang Ping-lin and Liu Shih-p'ei were also regular contributors. It was in this journal that Wang Kuo-wei first published his studies of the Chinese drama. Other publications of the association consisted of a monograph series containing reprints of some fifty titles of old manuscripts and books mostly by patriotic writers of the Ming and Ch'ing periods, and a series of textbooks compiled by Liu Shih-p'ei.[6]

In November, 1906, the association acquired a small brick building to house its hundred-thousand-volume collection of Chinese books, as well as visitors like Su Man-shu. The library was donated principally by Teng Shih and Huang Chieh, who also received generous help from other members and friends. In the various issues of the *Journal on Chinese Learning*, it was recorded that Man-shu contributed to the library collection on four occasions between 1908 and 1909. During his stay there in the fall in 1907, he joined the members of the association in a group picture taken in front of the library building. In this photograph, he appears as a dapper young man, dressed in a Western suit and wearing an overcoat and derby, and sharply contrasting with the staid, old-fashioned scholars in skullcaps and long gowns. With one of these men, Ch'en Ch'ü-ping, a fellow member of the Volunteer Corps in Tokyo in 1903, Man-shu formed a lasting friendship. Fellow lodgers in an upstairs room in the library, their two beds facing each other, the two men chatted congenially and pleasantly through the long nights of wind and rain. On another occasion, two out-of-town friends, Kao Hsü (Kao T'ien-mei) and Kao Hsieh, the former's young uncle, took Man-shu out to dinner in a restaurant where they feasted in the company of sing-song girls.

Otherwise, Man-shu's life in Shanghai was uneventful. Sometimes, he felt rather despondent and remorseful, as in the following letter to Liu San, written after a brief visit with Liu in Hangchow:

> To Liu San, my elder brother:
>
> I have not received any word from you since our all too hurried farewell. Could it be that you have found me unworthy of instruction and dropped me on account of my shallow nature and small capacity? How could I bear to be deserted by you so soon and so abruptly! For lack of experience, none of the things I did was right and proper; because of them I suffered estrangement from all my friends. How my heart aches when I think about it! Nevertheless, there is nothing easier in this world than to lay the blame on other people. That I have erred and have been living in misery, a very close friend like you certainly could not have failed to notice. Although I should not burden you with the troubles of my personal affairs, it breaks my heart every time I think of it.
>
> Alas! Liu San, I have no desire to sojourn in this foul and evil world! T'ai-yen [Chang Ping-lin] has written to ask me to accompany him on a journey southward to India. But at present, I do not have enough money for the trip and the date of our departure has not been set. Early next month I shall return to Japan. At this very moment, I have given up all social activities and only wish that you will not abandon me so much! The weather is cold and the winds are severe. Take good care of your precious self! Please instruct me whenever you have time. (*MSCC*, I, 197)

Man-shu went back to Japan in December, 1907, and soon fell sick. After leaving the hospital in Yokohama in early 1908, he resided with friends, mostly with Liu Shih-p'ei in Tokyo. Occasionally he visited Kawai; once he accompanied her to the seashore at Zushi. It was then that he spent much of his time reading Byron's poems, as well as English translations of Chinese poetry. Unfortunately, his peaceful life in Japan was upset by a bitter quarrel between Liu Shih-p'ei and Chang Ping-lin, the two most colorful members of his literary circle. It reached such an impasse that Man-shu had to move out of the Liu house, for Liu suspected him of siding with Chang.

It is perhaps worth mentioning that Liu Shih-p'ei's feud with his political and literary friends in Japan marked the beginning of his downfall. Embittered by disputes and goaded on by Ho Chen, Liu Shih-p'ei sold himself, in a desperate reversal of his revolutionary stand, to the Manchu government, whose emissaries had been active in recruiting, with money and promises of official position, Chinese intellectuals in Japan as spies on the revolutionists. In the winter of 1908, Liu Shih-p'ei went to Shanghai, where he continued his secret activities. He informed the government of the secret headquarters of a revolutionary group under Ch'en Ch'i-mei,[7] an important leader in the Kiangsu area, who was plotting an uprising in Shanghai; he also supplied the details of a clandestine meeting of insurrectionaries which he attended as a member of the China Alliance. This information led to the arrest of a number of lesser revolutionaries, Ch'en Ch'i-mei and the others having escaped.

By this time, Liu Shih-p'ei had reached the point of no return. Fearing revenge, he left for Nanking to serve as a personal secretary to the Manchu governor who had employed him in espionage work. After the death of this patron and the success of the 1911 Revolution, Liu Shih-p'ei lived in isolation from the outside world for some time. He returned to an active life again in 1915 as one of "six gentlemen-scholars" who urged the restoration of the monarchy and the coronation of Yüan Shih-k'ai as emperor. After Yüan's death in 1916, Liu Shih-p'ei once more found his position untenable and his livelihood threatened. It was then that Ts'ai Yüan-p'ei, a former friend, came to his rescue by appointing him professor of Chinese at National Peking University, where Ts'ai served as chancellor. Leaving a besmirched reputation as a political figure but a legacy of meritorious scholarship, Liu Shih-p'ei died shortly afterward in 1919, a year after Man-shu's death. Ho Chen, it is said, went insane soon afterward and still later shaved her head to enter a nunnery, thus completing the tragedy of this brilliant couple.

CHAPTER 4

The Wandering Poet-Monk

THE altercation between his two friends Chang Ping-lin and Liu Shih-p'ei further dampened Man-shu's already dwindling interest in politics. It also created the problem of having to find new quarters. He wrote to Liu San on May 7, 1908, that when the Lius shifted to him their wrath for Chang Ping-lin, he was thrown into a quandary: "I have already left them and am now roaming about without definite plans for the future. I would like to go back to Kwangtung, but alas, where can I get the money for the trip? So, I can only hold my alms-bowl and beg from door to door. . . . Every day I sit within these four walls of sorrow. As soon as I have raised enough money, I shall return to Lo-fou [in Kwangtung] to rest there quietly for a few months and then find some means to proceed on my journey southward [to India]. If I do not flee the rampant evils of this foul world, I will die of consumption!" (*MSCC*, I, 208). Henceforth, the self-image he nurtured was that of a frail poet-monk, often sad and forlorn, as in the following poem to Liu San (1910):

To be reborn in Heaven as a Buddha, I have no such aspiration.
Dark dreams vanish without a trace; my grief is extreme.
Thank you, Liu San, for inquiring after my health—
There still remains in me the lingering life of a poet-monk.

Saddened and discouraged by these experiences, a sense of resigned acceptance nevertheless persisted in his vision of himself. And it was this vision of life which informed the years 1908 and 1909, during which time he was most creative as a writer.

Between May and August, 1908, the *People's Report* published two medium-length serial works from his pen; namely, *Tales of Spectral Splendors on the Shores of Kwangtung* and a translation of *An Account of My Refugee Life on the Seashores of Sala* by the Indian author Ghocha. The last work was left incomplete when the *People's Report* was banned in Japan in November, 1908. Based mainly on his readings during the previous fall in the library of the Association for the Preservation of National Learning, the *Tales of Spectral Splendors* relates the stories of people in Kwangtung who preferred heroic death to abject servitude under the Manchu conquerors. Typical are accounts of scholars who led courageous life-and-death struggles against the enemy, or of other patriots who engaged in passive resistance by writing patriotic poetry. One story relates how a man named Li Cheng shaved his head to become a monk after his father's death in 1646, during the fall of their native city to the Manchu army. Li considered drowning himself in the sea, but then thought to himself: "I am only a cotton-clad scholar. Rather than follow my father [an official] in death, it would be better for me to live for the emperor. Were I to die with my father, he would lose his son forever and be dead indeed. Were I to live on as a subject of the emperor, I could still complete my span of life and fulfill my duties" (*MSCC*, II, 4). He then took off his cassock and returned home, where he led a quiet life, secluding himself in a small room. He did not practice Buddhist meditation. No one knew what he was doing. One day someone peeped in and observed that whenever he cut his hair, he wrapped it in a piece of paper; afterward, fully dressed and capped, he went into the mountains and burned it, wailing and crying all the time. When asked what he was doing, he replied: "I want to return my hair to my parents, but I grieve that I cannot return them my entire body" (*MSCC*, II, 4). The women in these tales likewise chose death rather than defilement by enemy soldiers. One of them, a beautiful concubine of a prince, after having falsely promised her abductor that she would surrender to him after her husband's burial, secretly placed several dozens of small knives inside her undergarments, the blades pointing outward and the man was stabbed to death as he held her in a tight embrace. She then killed herself with the same knives. These anecdotes are heavily colored by Confucian ideas of loyalty, filial piety, and chastity—attitudes which appear very rarely in the author's other writings.

A large number of these stories, particularly those of women, are taken from the works of Ch'ü Ta-chün, better known as Ch'ü Weng-shan, a Cantonese poet of the seventeenth century noted for his patriotic writings, many of which were banned in the Manchu period. After the fall of the Ming dynasty, Ch'ü Ta-chün left home to become a monk, but returned to secular life in middle age. It is natural therefore that Man-shu should have been attracted to his writings. Earlier, in the winter of 1907, he had conceived a plan to reprint and circulate in Japan a volume of *Women's Stories by Weng-shan*, taken from *New Stories from Kwangtung*. Kawai was to be designated as the sponsor of the project. Although these plans came to nought, he was able to incorporate some of Ch'ü's patriotic tales in the work published in the *People's Report*.

Little is known of *An Account of My Refugee Life on the Seashores of Sala* and its author beyond the information supplied by Man-shu. To lend a note of authenticity to the work, Man-shu retained a number of Sanskrit terms, such as *varsua* (rainy season), *varchika* (flowers growing in the rain), *cannas* (willow twigs), and *darca* (new moon), in the translation. References are made to the Code of Manu and the epic *Ramayana*, whose story may be summarized as follows:

> King Rama, accompanied by his wife Sita, traveled southwards after he had been driven out by his father. Once they went to visit Lanka [the Lion City]. Its king, Ravanna, struck by Sita's beauty, kidnapped her. Greatly enraged, Rama swore revenge. With a huge army he defeated and killed Ravanna, put the latter's younger brother on the throne, and recovered Sita. Consequently, the fame of King Rama's heroic exploits spread far and wide. Attracted by its culture, the Aryans migrated from Central Asia to the Southern Kingdom. (*MSCC*, II, 285)

The implications of these references to the *Ramayana* are that if Rama, the Indian hero-king, could fight to revenge his wife's abduction, the more reason therefore for modern Indians to revenge the defilement of their country by the British.

Ghocha's book deals mainly with the futile efforts of the Indian people to resist the British invaders, who are stigmatized as "big bandits." Likewise, foreign missionaries are said to dress in black and wear an object "in the shape of a crucifix that glitters like a butcher's knife." Indians who subserviently served the new masters are also denounced, but the severest attack is directed against the female sex in general: "Poisonous serpents harm the flesh, but women harm the spiritual body. They are full of jealousy; because of this, they are reincarnated after death among hungry ghosts. They are the messengers of hell and the sweet words they utter are poison" (*MSCC*, II, 282). This diatribe against womanhood is paradoxical, coming as it does from the mouth of the hero, whose wife is also the heroine of the story. These attitudes should not be taken, of course, as reflecting the personal sentiments of the translator.

Man-shu's aim in introducing this Indian story to Chinese readers is obvious. In the British conquest of India he saw a parallel to the subjugation of China by the Manchus. Denunciation of the British "bandit rulers" is coupled with the exaltation of the heroic resistance of the Indian freedom fighters. Their will to revenge was sharpened by a sense of humiliation, that of a great people suffering the loss of national identity and cultural heritage to which they clung obstinately and nostalgically. "You should know," said an elderly leader of the group, "our nation was the fountainhead of philosophy, in which we towered above Greece, which was a latecomer. Although our country collapsed early in ancient times, the others all learned from us and based their governments upon the Code of Manu, which regulates the people in peace and happiness. Alas! In this inferior generation, with the decline of our majstic power, we have gradually fallen into decay and today our magnificent and blissful land belongs to another people" (*MSCC*, II, 287). These sentiments touched a responsive chord in Chinese readers.

In the summer of 1908, *Affinities in Literature* (*Wen-hsüeh yin-yüan*) was published in Tokyo. Two volumes of this work were planned and advertised in the January issue (no. 15) of the *Tien Yee News*, but only the first volume was printed. According to the author, its publication was financed by an unidentified friend from Min-chiang (Fukien province). The two volumes constitute an anthology, mainly of English translations of Chinese poetry. The translations were not by Man-shu himself, but by English writers such as James Legge, Herbert A. Giles, John Francis Davis, George T. Candlin, and others. Man-shu's own contribution to the anthology consisted of a few translations from English as well as a number of paintings. Volume I contains translations of four poems from the *Shih-ching* by James Legge (*The Book of Ancient Poetry*, 1876); Li Po's poems by Herbert A. Giles (*Chinese Poetry in English Verse*, 1898); "The Maiden and the Flowers" by George T. Candlin (*The Chinese Fiction*, 1898); "The Tea-Picking Ballad" by W.T. Mercer, excerpted from *The Chinese Repository*, Vol. VIII, as quoted by John Francis Davis in *The Poetry of the Chinese*, 1870; and the "Ballad of Mu-lan" and the "Song of Everlasting Sorrow" by unknown translators. For comparison with Legge's translations, other English versions of the *Shih-ching* poems were also included, two each from Samuel W. Williams' *The Middle Kingdom* (1883) and Davis' *Poetry of the Chinese*. A relatively minor portion of the text is devoted to Man-shu's translations of a poem by Byron (which is quoted in Ghocha's *My Refugee Life on the Seashores of Sala*), Goethe's hymn on *Sakuntala* from E. B. Eastwick's English translation, and King Asoka's inscription on a monument to commemorate the Buddha's birthplace. A translation of Byron's "Maid of Athens" by a friend, Huang K'an, Chang Ping-lin's best-known disciple, was included under the pseudonym "The Mountain Man of Sheng-t'ang."

As an illustration of the intercultural flow between East and West, this anthology of translations from Chinese and Western poetry is aptly entitled *Affinities in Literature* and reveals one area of activity that was to develop in years to come. During one of his visits in Hong Kong, Man-shu became acquainted with the British missionary and scholar George T. Candlin, who showed him a translation of "The Maiden and the Flowers," namely, the flower-burial song attributed to Lin Tai-yü, the heroine of the Chinese novel, *The Dream of the Red Chamber*. The author's preface to *Affinities in Literature* refers to Candlin as "my teacher." This information suggests the interesting possibility that the study of English occupied Man-shu in the winter of 1903–4 when he was in Hong Kong. However, it is too slender a clue from which to pick up the threads of his life at that period. Candlin was a missionary in China and related his personal experiences in a book *On Service with the King* (1903), which consists in part of a collection of missionary sermons. Candlin's work on Chinese poetry was taken up after his death by his daughter, Clara Candlin, the translator of *The Herald Wind* (1933), an anthology of Sung dynasty lyric poems.

The preface to *Affinities in Literature* also gives ample evidence of Man-shu's interest in Byron, which began to grow in early 1908. From another source we know that during the months of February and March he did little else but read widely in Byron's verse, attempting to acquire, it would seem, a general rather than a detailed understanding of the Byronic spirit. A substantial portion of the preface is also given over to a discussion of the merits of the Sanskrit language and literature. The epics *Mahabharata* and *Ramayana*, the twin jewels of Sanskrit literature, and *Sakuntala*, the "sage-poet" Kalidasa's dramatization of the love story of the heroine, Sakuntala, with King Dusyanta, are mentioned in particular. According to Man-shu, it was William Jones's English translation (1789) of Kalidasa's play that inspired Goethe to write the hymn to *Sakuntala:*

> *Willst du die Blüthe des frühen, die Früchte des späteren Jahres,*
> *Willst du, was reizt und entzückt, Willst du was sättigt und nährt,*
> *Willst du den Himmel, die Erde, mit einem Namen begreifen,*
> *Nenn' ich Sakuntala, dich, und so ist alles gesagt.*

The Chinese version of Goethe's hymn, one of Man-shu's earliest attempts to translate Western poetry, contains eight lines of four characters each, and is rendered in a graceful and dignified style. Asserting once again the superiority of Indian philosophy and culture over the Greek, he wrote in the preface: "Sanskrit, I feel, combines simplicity and beauty of expression better than any language. Next comes Chinese. As for those barbarian tongues of Europe, they fall way behind" (*MSCC*, I, 121). This conviction he was to reiterate from time to time in later years.

In the same period, Man-shu published jointly with Chang Ping-lin two manifestoes on Buddhism: "An Admonishment of All Buddhist Disciples" and "A Manifesto to Both Officials and Commoners." These two articles constitute his most important pronouncements of religious faith, though both, as is to be expected, were influenced by his older and more learned friend. The "Admonishment" was addressed to Chinese reformers who advocated the conversion of Buddhist temples to modern, Western-style schools. While asserting the intrinsic virtues of Buddhism, the two writers admitted its degeneration in modern times, tracing the causes of decay to the vulgarity and worldly ambitions of the monks themselves. Some monks were said to frequent teahouses, gamble, and indulge themselves in sensual pleasures; others to hire themselves out for ritual performances; still others were admitted to seek the patronage of the rich and powerful for worldly gain. To remedy these ills, the writers urged a number of measures for the advancement of "Buddhist scholarship," namely, the study of the Sanskrit language, translation of the sutras, and, most importantly, further research in Chinese Buddhist literature for a fuller comprehension of the existing canons. On the other hand, they considered as deplorable the monks' spending their time on learning English, which was said to have only a secondary importance, and their looking toward Europe rather than India as the fountainhead of Buddhist lore.

In the second article, the authors demanded that government officials refrain from the confiscation of religious properties and establishments just because of the transgressions of a few law-breakers in the Buddhist community. They then launched into a long and spirited defense of the Buddhist faith against the accusations that as a religion Buddhism could not benefit the people's welfare and therefore should be abolished; that the monks were lacking in knowledge and virtue; and that the Buddhist Law, with its teachings of nonbirth and nondestruction, was meaningless in a modern society. The joint statement ended by urging the revival of Buddhist learning: "At present, in all schools, whether public or private, rules and regulations have become lax and ineffective. On the other hand, the restraining influences of Buddhist discipline, at least, are still operative in keeping its followers within bounds. If someone will engage in a revival of the Buddhist teaching, success can be easily expected."[1]

In the fall of 1908, Man-shu went once again to Shanghai and Hangchow where life seemed to be one of leisure and relaxation, instead of the busy literary activities and religious controversies of the Chinese resident in Japan. Once more he resorted to the peace and calm of West Lake and White Clouds Monastery, where he enjoyed the company of the resident monks Tê-shan and I-chou, the "superior men" as Man-shu called them. He also met Liu San briefly and received from him a small gift of money to replenish his constantly empty purse. Once again he considered a trip to India via Kwangtung province, but as usual he lacked the financial resources to realize this long-cherished hope. Instead, in October he accepted an invitation from Yang Wen-hui (Yang Jen-shan, 1837–1911), an eminent Buddhist scholar in his early seventies,[2] to teach at the Jetavana School (Chih-yüan ching-shê), which Yang had established in Nanking for the instruction of the priesthood in Buddhist scriptures. The school was located on the old site of Yang's Sutra Press, from which he had issued reprints of major Buddhist classics of the Mahayana School. Recruited from the monasteries in Nanking and neighboring cities, the students at the Jetavana School were taught Buddhist texts, Chinese, and English. Besides Yang Jen-shan, who lectured on the sutras, the faculty consisted of Li Hsiao-tun, a classical scholar, and Su Man-shu, the English instructor. In view of the sentiments expressed in his articles on Buddhism, it seems strange that Man-shu should have agreed to teach English instead of Sanskrit. His knowledge of the latter, however, was put to good use when Yang Jen-shan asked him to translate from Sanskrit two letters which an Indian monk, Dharmapala, had previously addressed to Yang. As the secretary of the Indian Mahabodhi Society, Dharmapala had visited Yang Jen-shan in 1893 and discussed with him, then and later in correspondence, the feasibility of an exchange program between Indian and Chinese monks. It was to prepare the Chinese monks for advanced study abroad that Yang Jen-shan started the school. Man-shu was understandably enthusiastic about the project, which he viewed as the fulfillment of a desire to restore Buddhism. "In two or three years," he wrote to Liu San, "if the monks should make good progress, they could be sent to Japan and India for advanced studies of the scriptures. Upon this effort, perhaps, depends the renaissance of Buddhist glories" (*MSCC*, I, 212). He himself gave four hours of instruction every morning and spent the rest of the day in meditation and attending sessions of scriptural exposition and preaching by the elderly Yang Jen-shan.

While employed at the Buddhist institute, Su Man-shu had a memorable meeting in November with Otto Franke (1863–1946), who was later to become a distinguished German sinologist. For twelve years an interpreter at the German legation in Peking, Franke returned to Germany from diplomatic service in 1901. There, he served as an advisor to the Chinese minister in Berlin from 1903 to 1909, during which time he became interested in Buddhism in China and Japan. On a trip to China in 1908, he was attracted by news of the Jetavana School in Nanking and stopped over to obtain firsthand information of this new Buddhist reform movement, which he recounted in an article a year later.[3] Besides discussions with Yang Jen-shan and the collection of materials on the Buddhist Institute, Franke also engaged Man-shu in conversations on Chinese Buddhist texts. In recording Franke's visit, Man-shu referred to him as a professor from Berlin University, although Franke's professorial appointment at the university was not actually made until much later in 1923. In their discussion, Man-shu was rather critical of Timothy Richard's translation of the *Ta-ch'eng ch'i-hsin lu* (*The Awakening of Faith in the Mahayana Doctrine*, Shanghai,

1907), one of the Buddhist texts used by the students at the institute. Man-shu also reported that he told Franke: "Everything in China has fallen into decay and ruin. No longer the Celestial Empire of yore, China will soon follow in the footsteps of India, Babylon, Egypt, and Greece" (*MSCC*, I, 125). These words apparently left little impression on the visiting German sinologist, who made no mention of Man-shu in his article on the Jetavana School.

His enthusiasm for the Buddhist Institute notwithstanding, Man-shu remained there barely three months. Before the year was out, he left Nanking for Shanghai, giving poor health as the reason for his departure. But aside from this one reference, at the time he complained no more to his friends about his illness. In a letter to Liu San, dated January 2, 1909, when he was about to leave for Japan, he wrote rather curtly in reference to the Institute, "I am not going back to Nanking again." Nor did he mention anything further about it. Like so many worthy projects of its kind, the Jetavana School was short-lived. Apparently, it failed to achieve the aims its venerable founder had envisaged for it, those which Man-shu had shared in the beginning. Nevertheless, it was important historically as a pioneer attempt by Chinese Buddhist scholars of the modern period to instill new life into Buddhism, to revive its teaching among both monks and laymen, and to rid it of ignorance and profane accretions.

Though Man-shu did not return to his work in Nanking and went instead to Japan, he had by no means lost interest in Buddhism. While in Tokyo in the spring of 1909, he was engaged by the Japanese Association for Sanskrit Studies as an interpreter for two Brahman monks from India, spending two hours in the morning and sometimes one hour in the afternoon on the job. Man-shu struck up an acquaintance with one of the monks that greatly benefited him in his Sanskrit studies. The two men conceived a plan to translate "The Cloud Messenger," a long poem by Kalidasa which Man-shu compared to Ch'ü Yüan's "One Encountering Sorrow" (*Li Sao*), but mental illness prevented him from carrying out the project. Also unsuccessful was an attempt, supported by Chang Ping-lin, Ch'en Tu-hsiu, and Kuei Po-hua, a follower of Yang Jen-shan, to set up a Sanskrit library. Nevertheless, something was accomplished during this period, for it was then that he began to read the *Mahabharata*. From it he learned that the name "China," meaning ingenious or crafty in Sanskrit, was first given to the Middle Kingdom by the Indians because of their admiration for the flourishing civilization of the Shang dynasty, corresponding in time to the reign of the great Indian king Bharata around 1400 B.C. Armed with this argument, Man-shu entered the controversy on the origin of the word "China" by opposing strongly the contention of some Western scholars and their Chinese followers that "China" was derived from "Ch'in," the Chinese dynasty of the third century B.C.

Man-shu's major accomplishment in 1909, however, was the translation of the *Selected Poems of Byron*, which he started in January immediately upon his return to Japan and before he became involved with the Association for Sanskrit Studies. A friend with whom he lived in a Tokyo temple during the winter recalled that Man-shu pleasantly whiled away his time translating the English poet. In the revision of this work, which was completed in May, Man-shu received the help of Chang Ping-lin, whose hand is clearly visible in the difficult and archaic expressions of some of these poems, especially "The Ocean" (from *Childe Harold's Pilgrimage*). It is doubtful, nonetheless, whether Chang's revision is an improvement over the original. Published in October, 1909,[4] the *Selected Poems of Byron*, a slender volume, contains such well-known pieces as "The Ocean," "The Isles of Greece" (from *Don Juan*), and "My Native Land, Good Night," as well as such shorter pieces as "To a Lady Who Presented the Author with the Velvet Band Which Bound Her Tresses," "Live not the Stars and the Mountains" (found also in *My Refugee Life on the Seashores of Sala*), and "The Maid of Athens." The last two poems were published previously in the *Affinities in Literature*.

There are two prefaces to the book: Man-shu's own in Chinese and an English preface by John B. Fletcher (1879–?). The date of Man-shu's preface, the thirty-second year of the emperor Kuang-hsü (1906), is unreliable. It is either a deliberate fabrication on Man-shu's part or a sheer mistake. The preface should have been written in 1909 (the first year of the emperor Hsüan-t'ung), because it mentions Man-shu's meeting with Otto Franke as having taken place during "the previous fall." Moreover, as has already been indicated, Man-shu did not read extensively in Byron until the spring of 1908, and he did not begin to translate in earnest until early 1909. One explanation for this discrepancy in dating could be that Man-shu, purposely ignoring the death of the Kuang-hsü emperor in the thirty-fourth year of his reign (1908), dated the preface in the late emperor's thirty-fifth year and by mistake it was printed as the thirty-second year. It could also represent a chance error by a printer's devil. In any case, it is most likely that the preface was written around September, 1909, when Man-shu was returning to Shanghai from Japan, and that the book itself was not published until a month or two later. Besides relating the episodes of his visit with Franke, the preface reveals his continued interest in the problems of translating from Chinese to English. On Byron, Man-shu's comments are brief but highly enthusiastic: "As a poet who conveyed in his songs the sorrows of departure from his own country and who would not claim any credit for helping the people of another country, Byron vied for glory with the sun and the moon" (*MSCC*, I, 125).

When in Shanghai in early October, Su Man-shu was first introduced to John B. Fletcher, an English poet-diplomat, by Ts'ai Shou. A long-time resident with the British consular service in China, Fletcher had acquired a love for things Chinese. At first, when Ts'ai Shou showed him an album of Man-shu's paintings, Fletcher was so favorably impressed by them that he wrote a poem of twenty-five lines, describing in rhapsodic terms the beautiful scenes depicted in these pictures:

> *Such gleams of nature, heart instilled desire,*
> *Such silent glory, cometary fire,*
> *Such mystic contemplation, raptured gaze,*
> *The artist's soul perceives, and limns in secret ways.*
>
> (*MSCC*, IV, 29–30)

Man-shu was naturally pleased with Fletcher's poem and presented him with one of his paintings, on which Ts'ai Shou inscribed a postscript dated October 7. The day before, Fletcher had also written the preface to the *Selected Poems of Byron*, in which he concluded: "For thousands of years isolated China has inherited undisturbed its ancestral characteristics: but as an organism which has grown quiescent may be rejuvenated by the assimilation of plasm from another cell, so the thought of a people may be refreshed by contact with new ideas. That Western and Eastern thought is producing this rejuvenescence in the Middle Kingdom can hardly be denied. The old monarchy of China is to acknowledge the vox populi as the vox dei. Nerves and fibres of democracy are shooting through this unsuspectedly republican mass."

Stating that the growing popular party requires a mental pabulum such as the native literature possesses but sparingly, Fletcher continued: "Mr. Mandju in translating for the Chinese public Byron's well-known 'Isles of Greece' and 'Good Night' has, we think, made a desirable addition to the literature of popular liberty in China; and can surely hope that the ideal thus presented will neither fail to find admirers nor to stimulate thought" (*MSCC*, IV, 32–33). As for Fletcher himself, his enthusiasm for Chinese art and poetry grew with the years. Later, while a consul at Hoihow (Hai-k'ou, a major seaport on Hainan Island), he published in Shanghai two volumes of translations: *Gems of Chinese Verse* (1918) and *More Gems of Chinese Poetry* (1919). They constitute the first important attempt to present systematically in English verse the poetry of the T'ang dynasty.

In return for the picture given to Fletcher, Ts'ai Shou presented Man-shu with a volume of Shelley's poems, a gift which Ts'ai received from Fletcher, who in turn had received it from a British lady. Later, when Man-shu showed this memorable book to Chang Ping-lin, the latter wrote on the volume rather facetiously the following words: "The original owner of this work was a woman. Through several changes of hands it finally came to the monk, Man-shu. However, if this should cause his fancy to run riot, as happened to Buddha's disciple Nanda, I wonder whether after all the gift is a blessing or a woe to Man-shu!" Knowing Man-shu as Chang did, his fears were well justified, for Man-shu inscribed the following poem to the British lady, whom he called "Miss Lily" (Lien-hua nü-shih),[5] in the same volume:

Who presented me with a volume of Shelley's melodious verses?
Alas! I have stumbled upon the tender trap of the heart!
I would like to repay this precious gift but have no way of doing it.
Faintly in a dream I perceive the familiar ripples in her eyes.

The same kind of wild romantic imaginings can be found in a group of poems written earlier by Man-shu to a "harpsichord player" while he was still in Japan. In that case, however, there was at least some kind of intimacy between the poet and the woman, as evidenced by the following poems composed while painting her portrait:

I

Collecting my Buddhist thoughts, I come here to wait upon her by the mirror stand.
Willow catkins, withered and smeared with mud, are doomed to lasting grief;
Thus, her harp strings are sprinkled with rouge-stained tears.
Flame and light, nonetheless, are reborn from the ashes of calamity.

II

Dabbing lightly her moth eyebrows, she comes to pay her respects to the master painter—
Her elegant hairknot, shaped like a twin heart, bound together by black silk.
Dipping my brush into a cup of water colors blended with two teardrops,
I paint a sprig of pear blossoms, but to whom shall I send it?

On another portrait of the harpsichord player—her name is cited as Momosuke—sent to Pao T'ien-hsiao (1876–), a former colleague in Soochow, he inscribed the following twenty-eight words:

Spring sorrows infinite and griefs immeasurable—
All at once resound through her finger-tips.
My cassock is already thoroughly wet,
How could I listen again to this heart-piercing harpsichord!

In another poem to the same lady, Man-shu asked:

How could I have the heart to paint idly with gold and powder,
When desolate woods and barren mountains dot everywhere my native land?

The identity of this so-called heavenly maiden, with whom Man-shu once had a flirtation, is unknown. It is possible that she was no more than a refined and talented geisha girl, who played the harpsichord to entertain guests. Some of the lines of these poems, particularly the reference to withered and mud-smeared willow catkins seems to confirm this hypothesis. If we should link the above allegory with the following stanzas from a group of "Occasional Poems," the allusion becomes more explicit:

Green jade[6] *has no reason to grieve about its origin, however humble it may be.*
A fairy from my native country, you alone have bewitched my soul.

The petals of cherry blossoms that dot everywhere my cassock
Are but one half rouge specks and one half tear stains.

* * *

In a high pavilion, too indolent to adorn herself, she sits playing the harpsichord,
Being ashamed to put on a fawning, simpering look for the vulgar lot.
All day long the gay quarters bustle and hustle without end;
While singing and dancing goes on in ten thousand houses, she alone lives a leisurely life.

In spite of his romantic relationship with the harpsichord player and other female friends, Man-shu always stopped short of any serious attachment, citing his Buddhist vows as reason for non-involvement. With a sense of finality, he thus addressed the harpsichord player:

After nine years facing the wall, I have attained an emptiness in form and mind;
How sad it is that I should have met you when I came back with a monk's staff!
For me, an ungrateful person, everything has now come to an end.
I'll just let the others enjoy the music of the harpsichord.

In a similar vein, he wrote:

I can only give back to you, dear maiden, an alms-bowl of unfeeling tears,
Regretting that I did not meet you before my head was shaved.

and:

Severing all ties of affection, voiding both form and appearance,
I shall lie asleep, with a sutra as my pillow, on the shores of Lake Biwa.

Located on the outskirts of Kyoto, this scenic lake was a favorite haunt where he withdrew to find peace and to refresh his fervid imagination.

The Japanese period between 1908 and 1909 was the most productive in his poetic career. In other poems written at this time, the usual themes of sadness and resignation are encountered, but new chords were struck as well. Passing the birthplace in Hirato of Cheng Ch'eng-kung (Koxinga), the famous Japan-born Chinese patriot of the Ming dynasty who led the resistance movement in

Taiwan against the invading Manchus, he mourned the dearth of heroes in modern times:

Travelers point to Lord Cheng's stone tablet at a distance,
Where white sands and green pines merge at the edge of the sunset.
I stretch my gaze towards the Celestial Empire, but the heroes have all gone;
In my cassock and in tears, I lie prostrate before the monument.

In a different vein, while traveling incognito in his monk's dress in the countryside, "with straw sandals and a broken alms-bowl," he recalled in a nostalgic mood the famous Ch'ien-t'ang tide near Hangchow. In this poem, as in a number of others, the beautiful scenery of rural Japan becomes even more lovely in Man-shu's verses:

Deep under the willow's canopying shadows the horse treads proudly,
Where a vast expanse of silvery sand pursues the ebbing tide.
The ice-flag atop a thatched store signals the nearby market;
The red leaves on the mountain top the lasses gather for firewood.
—Passing by Kamata

From this lonely village, dimly, dimly rises a wisp of smoke:
Everywhere the song of the sprouting rice as farmers toil in the field.
Riding a lean horse, I need not worry about the long road ahead—
The peach blossoms, so lovely red, yearn to come up to my singing whip.
—Singing on My Way to Yodoe

Thus it was that at the youthful age of twenty-six, Su Man-shu attained in his verse a manner of expression marked by a soaring imagination that cast a romantic spell over varying moods, little mementos, and the bittersweet experiences of life.

CHAPTER 5

The Southern Society and the South Sea Islands

THE poetic temperament and personal achievements of the author made him the center of an ever widening circle of literary men. When the Southern Society (Nan-shê) was founded in the winter of 1909 by K'ao T'ien-mei, Ch'en Ch'ü-ping, and Liu Ya-tzu, all personal friends, Man-shu joined it as one of its early members. By that time, he had already left Shanghai by way of Singapore to take up a teaching position at Surabaya, Java, but his absence from their periodical meetings did not deter his friends from communicating with him on the progress of the society, in whose journals were published most of his poetry and prose writings, including a number of letters written in the last ten years of his life. No wonder that Man-shu became known to posterity as a poet of the Southern Society. He was not its representative writer, but one of the best known and certainly the most popular.

The establishment of the Southern Society (1909–23), as we now view it, was an epoch-making literary event in modern China. From a mere handful of young intellectuals who first gathered on November 13, 1909, at the Chang Family Sacrificial Hall on Tiger Hill in Soochow, the society grew to be one of the largest associations of Chinese writers of all times, its membership increasing rapidly to more than one thousand at the height of its prosperity. While the society had its headquarters in the Yangtze region (Soochow, Hangchow, and Shanghai), its influence extended throughout the country. Besides regular spring and autumn gatherings in Shanghai, occasional meetings were held in Peking, Hangchow, Ch'ang-sha, and Canton. A semiannual publication of its members' literary contributions, the *Journal of the Southern Society* (*Nan-shê ts'ung-k'ê*), first issued in January, 1910, totaled twenty-three volumes (in twenty-two numbers) in the fourteen years of its existence; in addition, a volume of short stories was published in 1917.

The first revolutionary organization in the history of modern

Chinese literature, the Southern Society, so named in contradistinction to the "Northern Court" (Pei-t'ing) of the Manchu dynasty, aimed to disseminate through literary writings nationalistic ideas and sentiments and to promote the overthrow of the Manchu government. For this reason, it has been claimed that the Southern Society was a literary arm of the China Alliance, the grand union of revolutionary parties forged and led by Sun Yat-sen. This claim is true in the sense that the growth and decline of the Southern Society corresponded with that of the China Alliance, to which many members of the society belonged. In the years preceding the founding of the Chinese Republic (1912), these writers were fired with zeal for the revolution, despite its inherent dangers, and inspired by devotion to a common cause. That was the most fruitful period for both organizations. But just as discord was sown among the revolutionists as they jockeyed for position and power in the new government after the success of the revolution, so signs of a split began to appear about the same time in the membership of the Southern Society. The failure of Sun Yat-sen, Huang Hsing, and Ch'en Ch'i-mei in their campaigns against Yüan Shih-k'ai resulted in a crisis for the China Alliance; likewise, repercussions of the crisis were felt by Southern Society members and reflected in their writings, over which a mood of deep frustration and despondence began to settle. When the political stituation further deteriorated in the warlord period following Yüan Shih-k'ai's death, Southern Society members, having lost all hope and aspiration, gave up the struggle and whiled away their time in the ivory tower, occasionally sallying forth to seek the mundane pleasures of wine and women. Lacking a raison d'être, this once flourishing literary society barely managed to linger on for several more years until its inevitable demise.

Liu Ya-tzu (1887–1958), one of its three founders, later became the sole leader of the Southern Society, with which he was identified. Like the other intellectuals of his time, he was profoundly affected by two major political movements of the early twentieth century—the anti-Manchu revolution that culminated in the founding of the Republic of China in 1912, and the anti-Yüan Shih-k'ai and anti-warlord revolutions that led to the establishment of the Nationalist government in 1928. A typical man of letters of his time, Liu Ya-tzu had difficulty managing the practical affairs of life and politics, but he was a man of moral integrity and firm convictions, who would not bend or sway in the ill winds of political adversity and personal antagonism. An idealist, he believed in the ultimate triumph of socialism not only in China but throughout the world. He was probably alone among the Southern Society members who lived to acclaim the socialist revolution of the Chinese Communist party.

Born of a landholding bourgeois family in a small village in Soochow prefecture, he early imbibed the revolutionary ideas of Sun Yat-sen, of whom he remained a faithful follower. A young man barely in his sixteenth year, he went in 1903 to Shanghai, where he joined the Chinese Educational Association and the Patriotic Student Society, and was exposed to the insurrectionary ideas of Tsou Yung and Chang Ping-lin. In his second trip to Shanghai in 1906 he joined the China Alliance and gained the friendship of a number of similarly inspired and dedicated young intellectuals, including Kao T'ien-mei and Ch'en Ch'ü-ping. He was introduced to Man-shu in the same year.

These friendships were to be cemented later in the formation of the Southern Society, to which Liu Ya-tzu devoted virtually all his time from 1909 to 1918. In the latter year, his resignation from the leadership of the organization came about as a result of a controversy with other members, including Ts'ai Shou, over the relative merits of T'ang and Sung dynasty poetry. An upholder of the great traditions of T'ang, Liu Ya-tzu applied the same critical criteria to Ch'ing dynasty poets, among whom he showed a specific preference for K'ung Tzu-chen (1791–1841), a nineteenth-century patriot and reformer, over the poets of the T'ung-Kuang School,[1] who traced their inspiration to Southern Sung poetry. This literary dispute resulted in unpleasant personality conflicts, which in turn caused a deep split in the membership of the Southern Society. Although the organization continued for several more years, Liu Ya-tzu lost interest in it; instead, his literary activities turned in another direction, and he founded the New Southern Society (Hsin Nan-shê) in 1923. This not only supported the Nationalist party as the Southern Society had the China Alliance, but also advocated the use of the vernacular language as a medium of literary expression, a radical departure from the practice and conviction of Liu Ya-tzu's former friends. By that time, however, the literary world had been taken over by a group of younger writers, products of the May Fourth Movement, who had fewer inhibitions and a bolder outlook than the members of the Southern Society. Thus, after a brief period of revival, the Southern Society came to the end of its historical mission.

Twice in the first half of the twentieth century the political world of the new China was peopled by members of the Southern Society. Quite a few were catapulted into high positions in Sun Yat-sen's provisional government (1912) and later the Nationalist government (1928–49). In the early period, five Southern Society members, all young men of faith and enthusiasm, were appointed to the provisional government as vice ministers of interior, education, industry, communications, and justice. Two were appointed as secretaries to the president and one was elected vice president of the Senate. One of the secretaries was Liu Ya-tzu, who, according to his own account, stayed on the job for barely three days. The others left their posts when Yüan Shih-k'ai came to power. Later, in the Nationalist regime in Nanking and Chungking, all five major government organs were headed at one time or another by former members of the Southern Society.[2] For this reason it has been said, perhaps somewhat facetiously, that modern China represented the sphere of influence of the Southern Society. Su Man-shu, among whose friends were many future leaders of the Nationalist government, occupied a prominent place in these literary circles. Although these men attained political eminence long after his death, they continued to cherish a fond memory of the ephemeral but much beloved poet-monk.

On the other hand, Man-shu had less contact with those members of the Southern Society and China Alliance who became heroes of the revolution. He must have known Sung Chiao-jen, one of the leading contributors to the *People's Report*, and Ch'en Ch'i-mei, the military leader of Shanghai, but his acquaintance with them could not have been more than casual. Both Ch'en and Sung attended the Shanghai meeting of the Southern Society in September, 1911, on the eve of the great revolution, but Man-shu was far away in Java at that time. Later, like several other Southern Society members, Sung Chiao-jen and Ch'en Ch'i-mei met their deaths at the instigation of Yüan Shih-k'ai. The best-known military leader of the revolution and likewise a member of the Southern Society, Huang Hsing, was Su Man-shu's friend. Huang had been a fellow volunteer corpsman in Tokyo and a colleague at the Industrial School in Ch'ang-sha.

Apart from such eminent government officials and generals, the rank and file of the Southern Society, as would be expected, consisted of "cotton-clad" men of letters who distinguished themselves in poetry, prose, and classical scholarship. With only a few notable exceptions, the writers of the Southern Society constituted the most important group of intelligentsia of the time. It was through their talents and accomplishments that they came to dominate the Chinese literary world of the early twentieth century. Their influence, however, was due not so much to any special literary skill or expertise, though many of them were outstanding practitioners of their art, but to the vigorous ideas to which they gave voice. Without forsaking the time-worn medium of literary Chinese, the best writers of the Southern Society succeeded in re-instilling in it a new, refreshing vitality, thereby providing Chinese literature with a new direction and dedication. Examples of new vigor and effervescence in old-style poetry abound in the works of Liu Ya-tzu, Ch'en Ch'ü-ping, Kao T'ien-mei, and other Southern Society writers, but this cannot be said of the poetry of Su Man-shu, except for a few poems such as those entitled "Bidding Farewell to T'ang Kuo-tun" cited previously. For this reason, it may be argued that Man-shu, a poetic genius as he certainly was, fell short of becoming a major poet of the Southern Society.

Su Man-shu was closely connected, however, with this literary group. For him, the advantages of membership in the Southern Society were apparent. It helped to cement his relationships with former friends; furthermore, it widened significantly the literary circles to which he belonged at a time when he badly needed intellectual companionship and consolation. As has been mentioned earlier, Man-shu left Shanghai in the fall of 1909 to accept a position at Surabaya, passing through Singapore on his way there. The following letter addressed to Kao T'ien-mei on June 8, 1910, from Surabaya will serve as a link between this account of the Southern Society and the story of Man-shu's life:

Last year, when I returned to Shanghai from Yokohama, I intended to visit you at your fine study surrounded by the fragrance of cassia blossoms, but I failed to make the trip to your house. Not being able to sever myself from the roots of emotion, I was thinking anxiously of you when the first volume of the *Southern Society Journal* arrived a few days ago. I have been reading it day and night as if I were face to face with all my friends. Unutterable indeed are my joys! I find that my poor poems have been included in this collection.[3] Isn't this like heaping dung on the head of a Buddha?

Before I am aware of it almost a year has passed since I, this humble monk, traced my footsteps to these southern wilds, where my companions are medicine pots and stoves. Only recently I recovered from an old ailment. I have been spending these long days in chatting with farmers in the paddy fields or chanting poems, alone in a peck-sized room, to dispel my ennui. I couldn't help from heaving a long sigh when I came to the following lines:

Lately, after a long illness, I have been as light as a swallow;
My horse does not know when I am helped to the carved saddle.

Your own lofty compositions are unsurpassed in refinement and beauty. I greatly admire them. I have often said that Byron can be likened to Ch'ü Yüan and Li Po; Shelley matches Li Shang-yin and Li Ho; while Shakespeare, Milton, Tennyson, and the American poet Longfellow can only vie for a place with Tu Fu. That is why as national poets they are not to be compared with the great geniuses of the spiritual realm. Critics today maintain that the treasures of Western literature are all to be found in the old manuscript piles of Lin Shu and Yen Fu. Alas! How unflourishing is the literary spirit of our times! I have no chance to glance at Yen's translations and little time for Lin's novels, though I admire his rendering of *Cleopatra* [by H.R. Haggard] and *Robinson Crusoe*. During my youth I studied these two works in the original and so I bought the translations to read. *The Tales of Shakespeare* and *Nami-ko* are second-hand works. As Lin does not know English, his versions may be considered thirdhand, hence much inferior to the original. Translations is indeed a difficult task. Some time ago I read Ku Hung-ming's translation of "John Gilpin," which is quite close to the original in style and spirit. The English poem became famous because it was written overnight, and moreover it sings the praises of the king. How could one not be pleased with this extra flower on a fine piece of embroidery? However, Cowper did not write the poem for the common people, and it falls far short of the genuine and spontaneous utterances of our seven-step genius. It is unfortunate that Ku has little ambition for literature and confines himself to the work of a court versifier.[4]

In my opinion, anyone who wants to study the literature of another nation should first master its language. In times past, when Goethe met someone, he always advised him to study English, and specifically to read Byron's poems. Now, with Goethe's genius, he could very well translate Byron's poetry, but translation is no substitute for the original. If Li Po should be alive today, he would not challenge my words.

Last year when I sailed on the South Seas, I met Señorita Lopez, a talented young woman from Spain. She held a similar view and presented me with several volumes of Western poetry. In the midst of palm-winds and coconut-rains, whenever I trim the lamp and open a book to read, I think of Señorita Lopez without being able to forget her.

I wonder how you have been spending your time these days. Do you ever think of this poor monk adrift on this deserted island? Last night the merchants here invited me to a drink. I got so tipsy that I lay on the road until some friends came along to help me home before I woke up. This is the only ludicrous thing I have done since crossing the sea to this southern island.

(*MSCC*, I, 225–27)

A master of the epistolary style, this letter is as well written as it is important for an understanding of his attitudes toward poetry and translation, which will be discussed later.

Probably the questions of how Man-shu got the teaching position at the China Guild House (Chung-hua hui-kuan) in Surabaya, who provided him with an introduction, and why he accepted the post will long remain unanswered. We can only surmise that as a Cantonese, he must have had connections with his fellow provincials who populated Chinese communities abroad. It may even be possible that he was helped to this position by such members of the China Alliance as Feng Tzu-yu and others, although Feng makes no such claim in his reminiscences. This idea, however, is feasible because at that time the China Alliance was very active among overseas Chinese communities in setting up schools and newspapers for the advancement of the revolutionary cause. Feng Tzu-yu once told a story of the ridiculous deeds committed by an old-style Chinese gentleman whom he recruited and sent to teach Chinese at a school in the South Seas. Man-shu, who had traveled widely, of course, was a much better representative of the Chinese intelligentsia. Distance was of no concern to him if he found the trip worthwhile, which it apparently was from the financial point of view. In his case, he taught English, not Chinese, at the China Guild House in Surabaya. Though under Dutch rule, Chinese residents there evidently considered English important enough for their youngsters' education to have engaged a teacher.

Monetary considerations aside, the job would hardly have had any appeal for a man of Man-shu's nature and temperament. He disliked the climate, the general environment, and the people. He characterized Surabaya as a wilderness, a deserted island. In a poem to Chang Ping-lin, written about the same time, he complained about the weather: "Here the steaming heat hems me in this pent-up lodging;/Desolate and bleak are the South Seas!" But rather than the steaming heat, the "palm-winds and the coconut-rain," what troubled Man-shu most was the cultural barrenness of this Dutch seaport, his complete isolation from centers of Chinese literary activity, and the absence of sympathetic and congenial companionship. In the same poem to Chang Ping-lin, he wrote:

> *In my sleeves I have a brief message,*
> *Which I intend to send you by the blue bird:*
> *In my long journey abroad, I yearn for friends—*
> *This wish unfulfilled leaves me cold and depressed.*

If his poems and letters are an indication of his frame of mind at that time, his mood must have been pathetic indeed. This is shown in the following excerpt from another letter which he sent to Kao T'ien-mei and Liu Ya-tzu on June 23, 1910: "From this great distance, I have been thinking of you gentlemen in your gay parties, overflowing with wine and poetry, while here I drift about in this deserted island. Alas! How my ailing bones ache! Not knowing how many days I will survive,[5] how can I figure out the date of my return? . . . With all my best friends ten thousand miles away, I can't help feeling gloomy as I lay on my bed in deep contemplation" (*MSCC*, I, 228). After inquiring about Ch'en Ch'ü-ping and several other Southern Society friends, Man-shu concluded the letter with the following request: "You two gentlemen must have been very productive in your writings. I hope you will send me at your convenience a few samples to console me during my long, drawn-out illness" (*MSCC*, I, 229).

An interesting and singular episode in this period of his life was his relationship with Señorita Lopez (Lo-pi-shih), a fellow passenger on the boat to Singapore. By putting together several jigsaw pieces in his writings, one may reconstruct the various stages in the development of this affair to illustrate the curious workings of his fervid poetic mind. First, in the letter to Kao T'ien-mei, there is this brief but enthusiastic reference to the young lady, which speaks eloquently of mutual intellectual affinities and implicitly suggests her captivating charm. Next, we find in a poem, entitled "Inscribed on Byron's Poetic Works," the following note: " 'Hsüeh-hung' [Snowy Swan], a poetess from Spain, came to visit me on my sickbed and personally presented me with a lovely portrait of hers, a volume of Byron's poetic works, and a bunch of camellia flowers and sensitive plants. Very solicitously she urged me to make plans for a trip homeward. Alas! Early in my youth I shaved my head to learn the Buddhist Law but failed to accomplish anything. Whenever I think of my life, I have no words to express my pain. So, ill as I am, I write down these twenty-eight words on the front leaf of Byron's book. This sentiment will be appreciated only by Snowy Swan" (*MSCC*, I, 53). The preface, however, has little relevance to the poem itself, which becomes much longer in translation:

> *An autumn wind blows over the sea in the darkening twilight;*
> *Alone, I bewail Byron's fate as I pore over his poetic remains.*
> *You, poet, and I are wanderers, fluttering like reeds in the storm.*
> *May I beckon to your soul from across a strange land?*

The first line of the poem establishes the time and place in which it was written; in the note Man-shu gives this young lady a lovely Chinese name, "Snowy Swan."

We now turn to a long letter on Buddhism which Man-shu wrote "In Reply to the Scholar Chuang-hsiang [Chuang-hsiang ch'u-shih] in Madrid." In accordance with Chinese practice, the way in which "Chuang-hsiang" is used with "ch'u-shih" indicates that it is a first rather than a last name. There is no difficulty, therefore, in identifying "Chuang-hsiang" as being the personal name of a Spanish gentleman, to whom this letter was addressed. The letter, dated July 18, 1911, from Java, is an important article on Chinese Buddhist lore with its disquisitions on the historical origins of Buddhist rituals, the antiquity of Sanskrit, its relationship to Buddhist texts, and the fallacy, according to Man-shu, of identifying Ch'in, the ancient Chinese dynasty, with the name China. All are familiar topics found in his other writings. The letter also refers to the verses which Chuang-hsiang inscribed for Man-shu on his translation of *The Swallow's Letter*, a famous Chinese play of the seventeenth century. Unless we dismiss this Spanish gentleman as a figment of imagination, we are faced with some pertinent but inexplicable questions; namely, whether this letter was actually written to the "Scholar Chuang-hsiang"; if so, what kind of a Sinologist was this Spaniard who had such linguistic and intellectual capabilities as to be a qualified recipient of this erudite letter? One does not play on the zither for an ox, so the Chinese saying goes!

A still stranger account of the same episode is found in the following passages from the "Postscript to the *Voices of the Tide*," supposedly written by the Japanese monk Hishaku: "He [Man-shu] had once learned Western poetry from a Spanish scholar, 'Chuang-hsiang.' The latter wanted to marry him to his fifth daughter, Snowy Swan [Hsüeh-hung]. The monk wept and said: 'I have long dedicated myself to the service of Buddha. What else can I do but dishonor your order!' Then Chuang-hsiang equipped him for a trip to Siam. . . . He also translated *The Swallow's Letter* into English. Soon after he had completed the manuscript, Snowy Swan took it to Madrid with a view to publishing it in Europe" (*MSCC*, IV, 39, 41). These passages inform us that Man-shu not only completed the translation of *The Swallow's Letter* but also planned to have it published in Europe; also, that Chuang-hsiang, the Spanish scholar, once intended to arrange a match between Man-shu and his daughter.

In the novel *A Tale of the Lone Swan*, Lopez, a clergyman from Spain who lives with his wife and daughter in Hong Kong, becomes the English language teacher of the hero, Saburo. They also arrange to send the hero off to Japan. Before his departure, Señorita Lopez visits him, cordially holding his hand and presenting him with a bunch of violets and sensitive plants as farewell gifts, as well as several volumes in English, which turn out to be the complete works of Shakespeare, Byron, and Shelley (Chapter 7). Later, Lopez is identified as a native of Madrid (Chapter 19).

And, as if to further complicate the issue, Man-shu records elsewhere in personal notes and diaries, where there is no question of authenticity, that he received $200 from Madrid on August 20, 1912, and later, in an undated entry, another $460. Who but Lopez would have sent Man-shu such a sum of money, a tidy sum in those days, and what was the source of this income except possibly proceeds from the sale of the manuscript of *The Swallow's Letter*?

While there is much in this story of his relations with the Lopez family to strain one's credulity, it cannot be lightly dismissed as sheer fabrication. One is entitled, of course, to whatever interpretation one sees fit, but the truth, it seems, lies halfway between total acceptance and complete rejection. The former was the attitude of Liu Ya-tzu in 1928 when he published the *Complete Works of Man-shu*, but he moderated his view a few years later. The latter position is held by Henry McAleavy, the only Western scholar to have written on Man-shu,[6] who was apparently unaware of the diary entries.

While admitting that Man-shu's statements were sometimes compounded of fiction and truth, one can still piece together a fairly plausible story of his relationship with this cultured Spanish family. First, it is probable that Man-shu actually made the acquaintance of a Spanish gentleman, a Señor Lopez of Madrid, who had taken an interest in Chinese culture and Buddhism, and his daughter "Snowy Swan" on a boat from Shanghai to Singapore in the fall of 1909. It is also possible that Man-shu did fall ill at Singapore, hence, the episode of the young lady presenting him with flowers and books on his sickbed. The lack of any reference to her personal charms in his poem on Byron argues rather in favor of the contention that at that time he did not allow his imagination to run riot as he later did in Java. His letter to Kao T'ien-mei from Surabaya testifies to his fond memories of the young lady, whose loveliness must have increased with distance and time. A lonely bachelor on a remote island, it matters little that he had taken monastic vows and that his fancy roamed freely, thus giving rise to the happy illusion that he had once been offered the lady's hand in marriage!

In the meantime, it may be conjectured that Man-shu and his Spanish friends maintained correspondence at infrequent intervals. This encouraged Man-shu in his translation of *The Swallow's Letter*, which he finally sent to Lopez in late 1911, and which could very well have netted him the handsome amount of money received from Madrid. Unfortunately, the missing link, the translated play itself, has not been found.[7] As for the letter from Man-shu to "Chuang-hsiang," I am inclined to believe that it was not much more than a literary exercise, by means of which Man-shu paraded his Buddhist lore, with a reiteration of his pet ideas and favorite themes, to impress his friends in the Southern Society, in whose *Journal* it was first published.

Finally, the question remains, by what sort of magic did Man-shu transform the Spanish gentleman he met on the boat into an English teacher taking up residence in Hong Kong?[8] Here, for what it is worth, I would like to venture a new hypothesis. It is my view that in this instance Man-shu has grafted onto the story of his Spanish friends an early experience with a real English teacher, the Reverend George Candlin, and his daughter, Clara Candlin. Rather than the Lopez family of Madrid, it was the Candlins of Hong Kong who, as Man-shu's benefactors, might have helped send him off to Siam and Ceylon in 1904. On the other hand, the marriage offer, the most fantastic part of the Lopez episode, can be regarded as a case of phantasmagoria that served to satisfy the narcissistic ego of a delightfully naïve and sensitive spirit in the most trying period of his life.

To a poetic genius with a fertile imagination, melancholy and solitude may not prove to be entirely a bane, so far as literary creation is concerned. Left to his own resources and with little else to occupy himself during those long months in Java, Man-shu sought consolation in literature by reading the works of the English poets and those of his Southern Society friends. It was also one of the most productive periods of his life. Since leaving Yokohama in his teens, Man-shu had never lived as long in one place as he now did at Surabaya. Distance prevented him from making frequent trips back and forth between Java and Japan. Thus stranded on this "deserted island," he busied himself with serious reading and writing. As a result, he accomplished a number of projects: (1) *The Swallow's Letter*, previously mentioned; (2) *A Tale of the Lone Swan*; (3) *Random Notes from a Swallow's Mausoleum*; (4) *Names and Identifications of the Flora of the Western Hemisphere*; (5) *Modern Geographical Terms and Itinerary Charts for Fa Hsien's "Records of the Buddhist Kingdoms" and Hui Sheng's "Mission to the Western Regions."* Of these, the second and third works were published later in Shanghai and will be discussed in chapters 6 and 7 respectively; the last two have not survived. An announcement of the publication of the *Names and Identifications of the Flora of the Western Hemisphere*, renamed *A Botanic Treatise on the Flora of the Western Hemisphere*, as a joint undertaking by Man-shu and Lo-feng (Shen Yen-mou) was announced in the fifth and sixth issues (1914) of *The Republic* (*Min-kuo tsa-chih*) at a price of eight yen in Japanese currency. If the book was ever published, no copy of it is known to have survived. The manuscript of the *Modern Geographical Terms and Itinerary Charts* for the two Buddhist books of travel was probably sent to Kao T'ien-mei, who wrote for it a 476-word poem published in the second volume of the *Journal of the Southern Society* (July, 1910), praising Man-shu highly for this worthy effort:

The Reverend Man-shu, alone, has taken great pains in this work
To record the gradual spread of the true words of the Lord Buddha,
Drawing maps and providing comments as a guide to labyrinthine passages.
Who dare say that scholars today are not as good as those of olden times!
His notes reveal the truth like a string of pearls on an open palm,
So that his readers are given, as it were, a conducted tour of the Western regions—

In their minds hangs aloft the ensign of the Buddhist Kingdom;
Vividly before their eyes appear the magnificent offerings of gold and jade on Buddha's shrine.
(*MSCC*, V, 299–300)

After having made some sweeping attacks on the militancy of the Christian and Moslem religions, Kao T'ien-mei concluded the long poem by expressing his admiration for Man-shu's emancipation from worldly cares:

Discarding the impediments of wife and children like worn-out shoes,
Only a person like you could succeed in attaining non-involvement.
(*MSCC*, V, 301)

This passage is rather ironical when we recall that, unknown to Kao T'ien-mei, Man-shu was actually experiencing a kind of sentimental involvement in this period of his life.

While at Surabaya, Man-shu may also have undertaken the translation of Kalidasa's *Sakuntala*. It will be remembered that he highly praised this Sanskrit play and translated Goethe's hymn to it. In his Preface to the *Voices of the Tide*, he promised his readers: "Hereafter, I shall try my best to present them with a translation of the world-renowned *Sakuntala* by the famous poet Kalidasa of Hindustan, the Land of Lord Sakya Buddha" (*MSCC*, I, 131). Though the work is lost today, it is possible that Man-shu did complete the translation of *Sakuntala* shortly before the publication of *Voices of the Tide* in late 1911. In this connection, it should be observed that *Voices of the Tide*, his third publication following *Affinities in Literature* and the *Selected Poems of Byron*, is a work that likewise contributed to East-West literary relations. All three books were printed in Tokyo, but *Voices of the Tide* was larger and more beautifully printed than the other two. For its publication, he paid at least 420 yen, according to the expense account kept in his diaries. He personally saw to its publication when he returned to Japan by way of Canton in May, 1911, his only trip out of Java during his stay there.

In addition to a portrait of Byron, *Voices of the Tide* contains two pictures of Man-shu himself, one in Western dress and the other in Buddhist garb with the legend "The Monk Man-shu, taken in the Kingdom of the Lions [Ceylon]." In both, Man-shu looks young and handsome in sharp contrast to another picture taken at Surabaya in the spring of 1910, in which he impresses one, with his dark glasses and long beard, as a sophisticated man of the world. The book is divided into two parts. Part I contains translations from English to Chinese, and vice versa. It includes all the translations of Byron that had first appeared in *Selected Poems*, as well as translations of "A Red, Red Rose" by Burns, "Departure of the Swallow" by Hewitt, Shelley's "Song" ("A widow bird sat mourning for her love"), "Sakuntala" by Goethe, and "A Primeval Eden" by the Hindu poetess Toru Dutt (1890–1908). A few Chinese poems translated into English were taken from the works of Western translators. Part I also contains "A Chronology of Byron's Life" compiled by J. B. Fletcher. Part II comprises an anthology of forty-two poems by British poetesses compiled by Man-shu and "personally copied by Snowy Swan, a Spanish lady, while she was traveling in the Southern lands."

The poet's English preface to *Voices of the Tide* discusses at large the life and poems of Byron and Shelley. His only known writing in English, the preface represents not only his views on the two British poets but also his English style; for this reason it is quoted here in its entirety, except for three short paragraphs at the end:

Byron and Shelley are two of the greatest British poets. Both had the lofty sentiment of creation, love, as the theme of their poetic expressions. Yet, although both wrote principally on love, lovers, and their fortunes, their modes of expression differ as widely as the poles.

Byron was born and brought up in luxury, wealth, and liberty. He was an ardent and sincere devotee of liberty—yes, he dared to claim liberty in every thing—great and small, social or political. He knew not how or where he was extreme.

Byron's poems are like a stimulating liquor—the more one drinks, the more one feels the sweet fascination. They are full of charm, full of beauty, full of sincerity throughout.

In sentimentality, enthusiasm and straight-forwardness of diction, they have no equal. He was a free and noble hearted man. His end came while he was engaged in a noble pursuit. He went to Greece, where he sided with the patriots who were fighting for their liberty. His whole life, career and production are inter-twined in Love and Liberty.

Shelley, though a devotee of love, is judicious and pensive. His enthusiasm for love never appears in any strong outburst of expression. He is a "Philosopher-lover." He loves not only the beauty of love, or love for love, but "love in philosophy" or "philosophy of love." He had depth, but not continuance: energy without youthful devotion. His poems are as the moonshine, placidly beautiful, somnolently still, reflected on the waters of silence and contemplation.

Shelley sought Nirvana in love; but Byron sought Action for love, and in love. Shelley was self-contained and quite engrossed in his devotion to the Muses. His premature and violent death will be lamented so long as English literature exists.

Both Shelley and Byron's works are worth studying by every lover of learning, for enjoyment of poetic beauty, and to appreciate the lofty ideals of Love and Liberty.

(*MSCC*, I, 130–31)

As there is no mention whatsoever of *Voices of the Tide* in this preface, some critics are of the opinion that it was originally written for the *Selected Poems of Byron*. This belief is strengthened by the short paragraph immediately following the passages quoted above: "In these pages, I have the honor to offer my readers translations of a few poems from the works of Byron" (*MSCC*, I, 131). I would like to suggest the possibility that this preface, once intended for publication in the *Selected Poems of Byron*, was withdrawn in favor of Fletcher's preface to the same work when it was given to Man-shu in early October, 1909. By that time the *Selected Poems* was ready to go to press and there was no space in it for a few extra pages. So the only thing Man-shu could do was to print Fletcher's preface in place of his own, both being approximately of the same length. Now he found a use for his preface in *Voices of the Tide*.

According to the title page, *Voices of the Tide* was copied and collated by the Japanese monk Hishaku. For this service, the latter probably received eighty yen from Man-shu in two installments of forty yen each. Hishaku, it will be remembered, was the supposed author of the "Postscript" mentioned above. Strangely enough, the "Postscript" was not included in the book itself but appeared a year later as an article in a newspaper supplement in Shanghai. By that time Man-shu had already left Java for a new life quite different from his intellectual isolation but furious literary activity in Java.

CHAPTER 6

The Lone Swan

THE glad tidings of the 1911 Revolution reached Su Man-shu in remote Surabaya amid an atmosphere of general excitement and exaltation that prevailed everywhere among Chinese people at home and abroad. After more than ten desperate attempts, and many losses and sacrifices, to overthrow the Manchu regime, the revolutionary forces finally succeeded in establishing themselves in the Wu-han area in Central China. Throughout the nation, reaction to the revolutionary movement was favorable and positive. In Shanghai, insurrectionists under Ch'en Ch'i-mei wrested the Woosung Arsenal and the Chinese city north of the foreign concessions from government control. Their victory sparked uprisings in other key cities in Kiangsu and Chekiang, the two fertile lower Yangtze provinces, and led to the capture of Nanking by revolutionary forces. These activities were climaxed by the arrival of Sun Yat-sen in Shanghai on December 25. A week later, on January 1, 1912, the Republic of China was born, and Sun Yat-sen was elected its first president at a convention of provincial delegates gathered at Nanking. Not long afterward, Su Man-shu also found his way back to Shanghai, not as a revolutionary follower but as a celebrated man of letters.

The first indication of Man-shu's response to the overthrow of the old regime can be found in a letter sent from Java to Ma Chün-wu and Liu Ya-tzu on December 18, 1911: "Now that the Heavenly Voice of our Great China has been aroused, I imagine both of you are talking excitedly, clapping your hands under the shadows of the glittering swords. Here in this strange, remote country I can only send my spirit to join you" (*MSCC*, I, 238). Anxious to return to China, he tried to raise money for the homeward journey by pawning his books and his black "swallow-tail suit." Teaching duties at school, however, prevented him from taking the trip until February, 1912. A month later he reached Shanghai after a brief visit with Huang Chieh and Ts'ai Shou in Canton and a stopover in Hong Kong, where he would have been stranded had it not been for the generosity of his elder cousin Su Wei-han, who lent him five hundred dollars to resume his journey. Once in Shanghai, he stayed with Liu Ya-tzu at the offices of *The Pacific News* (*T'ai-p'ing-yang pao*), located on newspaper row in the International Settlement. It was in the same city almost nine years before that he had started his career as a journeyman translator for the *National People's Daily*, and once again he associated himself with the newspaper profession as a contributor of occasional articles for the literary section of the paper, which Liu Ya-tzu edited.

Because of early exposure to Western influences, Shanghai had long been a major center of Chinese journalism. In particular, the foreign concessions afforded a haven for radical writers from persecution by the government. Even though Chang Ping-lin and Tsou Yung, as will be recalled, were ultimately jailed in the British concession for antigovernment propaganda, they could easily have been beheaded had it not been for the refusal of the foreign authorities to hand them over to Chinese government officials. With the establishment of the Republican regime south of the Yangtze River, the revolutionaries found in Shanghai an even more fertile ground for the propagation of their ideas. They could do so now without interference or threat to life and livelihood. As a result, a large number of newspapers and periodicals representing a wide range of political coloration thrived in Shanghai in the 1910's.

Revolutionary party newspapers published in Shanghai numbered at least ten, among which may be mentioned *The Pacific News, Heaven's Bell (T'ien-to pao),*[1] *People's Stand (Min-li pao), People's Right (Min-ch'üan pao), People's Voice Daily (Min-sheng jih-pao), Divine State Daily (Shen-chou jih-pao),*[2] *Great Republican (Ta kung-ho pao), People's National News (Min-kuo hsin-wen),*[3] and the *Times (Shih-pao)*. Of these, the *Times* alone survived to become a major newspaper, but only by changing its focus principally to commercial news with little political reportage. The most important paper of a transient nature was the *People's Stand*, the official organ of the China Alliance, which was edited by Sung Chiao-jen in the pre-Republican era. Many editors of these papers, like Sung, were also members of the Southern Society. This was particularly true of *The Pacific News*, which was completely staffed by society members from the publisher and editor in chief, Yeh Ch'u-ts'ang, to bureau managers. Among its dozen or so editors were Liu Ya-tzu and a new arrival, Su Man-shu.

Typically, Man-shu did not stay long on the job. Having barely shaken off the dust of his long sea voyage, he took a side trip to Hangchow. Then at the summons of Kawai, he left for Japan in late April. He returned to Shanghai a month later only to return again to Japan soon afterward. There he remained four and a half months from mid-June through October, when he retraced his steps to Shanghai. During this interval, the internal situation in China had greatly deteriorated. With the vain hope of effecting peace and unification in the country, Sun Yat-sen had resigned the presidency in favor of Yüan Shih-k'ai, who, once entrenched in power, began to rid his government of revolutionary leaders. The ill winds of politics blew away the erstwhile enthusiasm and exaltation of the younger revolutionaries. In October, 1912, *The Pacific News* too folded for lack of financial support.

Although his connection with the paper was brief and intermittent, Man-shu published in it ten poems, three articles, a letter, the "Postscript to *Voices of the Tide*," and, most important of all, *A Tale of the Lone Swan*, which appeared in serial installments from May to August. On May 28 it was announced that, having newly arrived from Japan, Man-shu was about to publish "Three Hundred Poems, Without Titles" in the paper. However, these poems never appeared in print, and presumably they were never written. Among his poetry that did appear in *The Pacific News*, only two were of recent date; most of the remainder had been set to paper in 1909 in Japan and have been discussed in a previous chapter. The following poem, composed in early 1912 on the eve of his departure from Java, adds another reason for his urgent desire to return to East Asia:

Fan P'ang had a mother whom he was duty-bound to support;
How could Chang Chien consider as homecoming his floating life?
Even to dream of this ten-thousand-mile journey saddens my heart.
At this southern land I bid you farewell, the tears coursing down my robe.
—Parting from Mr. Chang at Java[4]

The first of the three articles, entitled "A Talk on the South Seas," protests Dutch mistreatment of Chinese settlers in Java and expresses the pious wish that the newborn Republic would not desist in its efforts to negotiate with the Dutch government until all its tyrannical rules were abolished. Another article is a personal impression of the performance of a well-known Shanghai actor, favored by Liu

Ya-tzu. The third, while relating the events of his recent visit to the Shanghai Famine Relief Bazaar sponsored by Chinese and foreign nationals, also contains caustic remarks on the dress worn by "modern" Chinese women. After having praised the charitable deeds of male and female visitors to the bazaar, he wrote:

> There is only one drawback. Many of our female citizens seen at the bazaar were dressed in an uncouth and unbecoming manner. They were very much pleased with themselves and considered themselves "civilized" in this way. This humble monk, however, very respectfully advises them not to ape the foreign fashion of revealing their high bosoms and slender waists, but to adopt as a motto on their dressing stand: "A refined and modest girl marries not for her looks but for her virtue." (*MSCC*, I, 167)

Rather controversial but extremely interesting and useful are the contents of the "Postscript to *Voices of the Tide*," a work attributed to Hishaku, but actually written, in the opinion of most critics, by Man-shu himself. This is not to deny the existence of a Japanese monk by that name, one who did in fact aid Man-shu, as has been indicated above, in preparing *Voices of the Tide* for publication, but to argue against his authorship of the "Postscript," which to all intents and purposes is an account of Man-shu's own life. Most likely written in the summer of 1911 in Japan, the "Postscript" was excluded from the printed version of *Voices of the Tide* for obvious reasons. Instead, he gave this handwritten document a year later to Liu Ya-tzu, who had it published in the literary section of *The Pacific News*, June 9–13, 1912.

A careful examination of the "Postscript" reveals that, except for two major discrepancies, it agrees in the main with our present knowledge of Man-shu's life. It gives a long list of the teaching positions he held at schools in Soochow, Ch'ang-sha, Wu-hu, Nanking, Surabaya, and other places, and an enumeration of his works written before 1912. The first list has been verified by the testimony of several colleagues and students who knew him in these educational institutions and by his own letters that have been preserved. The second list is eloquent testimony to the productivity of this promising young man of twenty-eight. To be sure, it contains a number of items that are no longer extant, but their disappearance need not cause us to cast doubt on the veracity of the list itself. A typical instance is the *Sanskrit Grammar*. While it was not written in the sanctuary of a famous monastery outside Hangchow, as claimed in the "Postscript" and elsewhere, there is evidence that he did compile this book in a rather prosaic environment, namely, a combined editorial office and lodging in Tokyo. As has been mentioned previously, we have today the prefaces to the *Sanskrit Grammar* by Chang Ping-lin and Liu Shih-p'ei; an advertisement in the *People's Report* (fifteenth issue) and the *Tien Yee News* (sixth issue) of the same work with a detailed table of contents of the first volume; Ch'en Tu-hsiu's testimony, corroborated by Chang Ping-lin in the first version of his preface to the *Sanskrit Grammar*, as to Man-shu's familiarity with the English works of Friedrich Max Müller and Monier Monier-Williams, which Ch'en Tu-hsiu purchased and gave to Man-shu for reference; Man-shu's own preface to the *Sanskrit Grammar* and his letters to Teng Sheng-hou, a colleague at Wu-hu, and Liu San, written from Japan in July and August, 1907, respectively, in which he informed his friends of its impending publication, enclosing in each envelope a copy of the announcement. Such a wealth of incontrovertible evidence can hardly be brushed aisde even by the most skeptical.[5]

On the other hand, the "Postscript" should be used with great care as source material for the reconstruction of Man-shu's life. It contains a number of errors—inventions, omissions, and inflated statements—that can easily entrap the unwary biographer.[6] First to be noted is his attempt to lend, as he had been doing all his life, an aura of dignity and solemnity to his status as a Buddhist monk.[7] In this instance, he put himself in the cassock of another monk, Po-ching, who died shortly after Man-shu had become a novice at a dilapidated temple in Hui-chou. Somehow or other, Po-ching's ordination certificate, issued by the Monastery of the Sea Clouds (Hai-yün szu), fell into Man-shu's hands.[8] Armed with this document, he now claimed that he had been given the Buddhist name Po-ching at the time of his initiation at the Monastery of Longevity (Ch'ang-shou szu) in Canton by a master monk from the Monastery of the Intelligent Dragon (Hui-lung szu), and that later he received grand ordination at the Monastery of the Sea Clouds on the Thunder Peak (Lei-feng) in Canton prefecture. Equally inflated is the account of his formal education, which, according to the "Postscript," consisted of two years of Western art education at Uēno and three years of instruction in political science at Waseda. Understandably, Man-shu preferred not to mention his schooling at Ta-t'ung, the

Yokohama educational establishment of the K'ang-Liang faction, which at that time was anathema to his revolutionary friends. The story in the "Postscript" of Chuang-hsiang's offer to marry his daughter to Man-shu has been discussed in the previous chapter.

Most baffling to his biographers as well as to his friends who first read the "Postscript" in *The Pacific News* is the account of his parentage. Here he presents himself as a person of Japanese ancestry named So-nosuke. He states that his father died in his infancy and that he was brought up by his mother, Kawai, in Tokyo. "At age five," he continues, "he left his mother to journey westward to China with a distant relative. While there, the latter conducted his business on the southern coast. The boy was given a new name, Su San-lang [Saburō], and the courtesy name Tzu-ku. It was then that he began to learn the Cantonese language" (*MSCC*, IV, 38). In a later passage, Man-shu's grandfather appears as Tada-o. While this account is startling enough, it corresponds amazingly well with the story in *The Lone Swan*. Here the father of the hero Saburō is said to be a Japanese man, Mūne-o, who came from a well-known clan in Tokyo. He died when Saburō was only a few months old. Later, "in order to transplant his roots in the soil of a superior nation," his mother, who is later identified as Kawai, adopted the boy out to a Chinese friend of his father so that he could "rid himself of the embedded nature of the island people to grow up like a dragon among men" (Chap. 3, *MSCC*, III, 14). Holding the boy in her arms, she went secretly to China and sojourned there for three years before returning alone to Japan. The "Postscript" and the novel were written in the same period of his life, and it is more than mere coincidence that they should contain almost identical stories of his Japanese origin, the only difference being the episode of Kawai's trip to China which is found only in the novel. The "distant relative" in the first account and the "father's friend" in the second were apparently one and the same person, a Chinese man from Kwangtung province.

While the story in *The Lone Swan* can be dismissed as fictitious, the biographical account in the "Postscript" is too important to be brushed aside as completely unfounded. A number of critics, including Liu Ya-tzu, have been led to conjecture that Man-shu was actually the foster son of a Cantonese merchant in Japan, surnamed Su, and that both Man-shu's parents were Japanese. This theory gained wide circulation and support when Liu Ya-tzu and Liu Wu-chi introduced it in the *Chronological Life of Su Man-shu and Other Articles* (1927) and the *Complete Works of Man-shu* (1928). Soon afterward, however, through the help of Feng Tzu-yu, Man-shu's earliest known boyhood friend, Liu Ya-tzu located the Su family at Li-ch'i village in Hsiang-shan county and initiated in 1928 a lengthy correspondence with its members, particularly Su Hsü-t'ing, Man-shu's elder brother, Su Wei-lu, his cousin (the youngest son of his father's younger brother), and Su Shao-hsien, his nephew, the son of Su Hsü-t'ing. This led to many important findings on the family background and early life of Su Man-shu. The results were so fruitful as to make it possible for Liu Ya-tzu to compile a genealogical table of four generations of the Su clan, from the patriarch Su Shih-ch'ang, Man-shu's grandfather, down to Man-shu's inferior generation (*see* Appendix I).[9]

While members of the Su family agreed unanimously in repudiating the idea of his having a Japanese father, Su Wei-lu, who was close to Elder Ch'en-shih, revealed that Man-shu was born not to Kawai but to Owaka, a Japanese maid. Over Su Hsü-t'ing's objection, Liu Ya-tzu accepted the story[10] and incorporated it in his revised biography of Su Man-shu (*see* Appendix II), which in turn has been accepted since then by most writers. It has been suggested that Kawai probably hid this fact from Man-shu, who therefore had no knowledge of his real origin, but that he was suspicious enough to create a legend of his own, that of his complete Japanese parentage, which was incorporated in the two works mentioned above. These he wrote at a moment when his fervid mind, beset by doubts and suspicions, imbued his writings with all sorts of fantastic ideas. In a more sober moment, he withdrew the "Postscript" from *Voices of the Tide*, but later gave it to Liu Ya-tzu for publication in *The Pacific News*.

Whatever one's evaluation of the "Postscript" as a biographical document, it is a fine specimen of Chinese prose. Of even greater literary value is the *Tale of the Lone Swan*, a work of sensibility and delicate sentiment that has deeply moved readers ever since its initial appearance in the first year of the Republic. According to Hu Huai-ch'en (Hu Chi-ch'en), another of his Southern Society friends who succeeded Liu Ya-tzu as editor of the literary section of *The Pacific News*, the novel first appeared in a Chinese newspaper in Java sometime between late 1911 and early 1912, but only the first few pages got into print before the paper ceased publication.

Later, it was serialized in *The Pacific News* for almost three months from May to August, 1912. When *The Pacific News* closed, Hu Huai-ch'en took the manuscript with him and kept it until 1919 when he reissued it in book form. Since then it has been widely reprinted and rendered into three foreign languages: two English translations by George Kin Leung (Shanghai, 1924) and Henry McAleavy (an abridged translation in his *Su Man-shu, a Sino-Japanese Genius*, 1960), a Japanese version by Iizuka Akira (Tokyo, 1938), and a German version by Anna von Rottauscher (*Der Wunde Schwan*, Vienna, 1947). In 1925 a dramatized version of the novel, compiled by Huang Chia-mu, a schoolteacher, was performed by the students of Amoy University in Fukien.

In its present form *The Lone Swan* is incomplete, although it is quite certain that it is all that Man-shu actually wrote. This can be explained by the fact that the novel was left unfinished when Man-shu hastened back to Shanghai from Java in early 1912. While shuttling back and forth between Shanghai and Tokyo in the same year, he must have been so distracted by numerous other activities, literary and social, that he had neither the time nor the inclination to bring it to completion. Quite likely, he himself had no idea of the ultimate fate of "the lone swan" in its hapless wanderings in this floating world. One thing, however, seems to be certain. The novel was bound to end, as it did, in tragedy.

The story of *The Lone Swan*, then, is the tragedy of a young hero, Saburō, a sinicized Japanese, torn by conflict between his desire to emancipate himself from worldly ties and emotional entanglements and to attain serene peace as a monk, to which life he has dedicated himself, and the ensnaring influences of female love showered upon him by the gentle and kind souls in his company. It is easy to endure the personal cruelty and oppression of family personified by Saburō's stepmother; sufferance is painful but endurable. On the other hand, courage and resoluteness are required to untangle one's self from the web of love. Such is Saburō's problem. The tragedy arises when he decides to rescue himself from drowning in a sea of human kindness in which he has been submerged. In a critical moment, he realizes how his actions, strictly proper and well intentioned from his viewpoint but nevertheless self-centered and selfish, have wounded to the quick those loved ones who have given him their heart.

In his adventures he encounters two fair and intelligent young women: Hsüeh-mei, his Chinese fiancée, and Shizuko, a Japanese girl, the daughter of his mother's sister. In the first episode, which takes place in a small village in Kwangtung, Saburō's foster father and Hsü-mei's father, being fellow villagers and good friends, arrange their children's betrothal to strengthen their own relationship, but Hsüeh-mei's family retracts the contract after the death of Saburō's foster father. To free Hsüeh-mei from her obligations, Saburō takes the decisive step of becoming a Buddhist monk, which, however, wounds his fiancée's sensitivities. Social conventions prevent the young couple from meeting, but, in a chance encounter with Hsüeh-mei's maid, Saburō is given a letter from her mistress:

> Blending my tears with ink, your handmaiden Hsüeh-mei curtsies on presenting this letter to you, Saburō:
>
> "Formerly, people all said that you had shaved your head to live in the hollows of the mountains. As you are endowed with an independent and steadfast nature, I believe in their words. Often I cry out in grief until my very breath almost ceases. On silent nights my thoughts often wander after you, but the road thither is indistinct in my dream."
>
> (Chap. 5, *MSCC*, III, 27)

Such steadfastness of purpose could only be found among the young in conventional China where people took seriously their childhood troth. After reiterating her constancy to him, she continues:

> "Alas! Saburō! Unfalteringly, I shall keep forever in my heart our eternal vow. If some day I should be forced by my parents to remarry, I could have at least one recourse: to kill myself to prove my faith. Even though my bones may decay and my body waste away, I will remain united with you in heart for countless ages." (Chap. 5, *MSCC*, III, 28)

Hsüeh-mei's words forbode tragedy; near the end of the novel, when Saburō returns to China after an eventful visit with his mother in Japan, he is told the news of Hsüeh-mei's death from a broken heart. He returns to the village in Kwangtung but fails to find her grave among the desolate mounds of a village burial ground.

Saburō's trip to visit Kawai, his Japanese mother from whom he has been separated since childhood, is made possible through the generosity of Hsüeh-mei, who had sent him one hundred dollars for traveling expenses. He is also assisted by the Reverend Lopez, a Spanish missionary in Hong Kong. The reunion between mother and son at Kawai's house in Zushi near Yokohama is an occasion of supreme joy that ends in tears. On the other hand, the visit to Saburō's aunt at Hakone, where Saburō first met Shizuko, turns out to be a prelude to another heartrending tragedy. Their love at first sight contrasts sharply with the kind of conventional, stereotyped attachment arising from the marriage contract that bound Saburō to Hsüeh-mei. The tender scenes between Saburō and Shizuko, somewhat marred by suspicion and remorse, are sprightly, exhilarating, and vibrant with emotion and pathos. While staying with his aunt, Saburō has a memorable meeting with Shizuko one evening in front of their seashore bungalow in the waning moonlight.

> With an agitated heart, I turned slightly away from where Shizuko stood. Pointing to the vast sea beyond, I said deliberately in a casual voice: "My elder sister, look there at that dark speck in the heart of the sea. Could it be a small fishing boat that's coming toward us?"
>
> Shizuko hung her head without uttering one word. After a short while, she came closer to me, the waves of her eyes gleaming softly upon my face. Under the misty haze of the moonlight, I gazed intently but quietly at her countenance, which, like a slanting moon in a cluster of clouds, appeared extremely serene and beautiful. At this very moment, all sounds were hushed but for the throbbings of my heart. Then, as I raised my head to look at the sky, I noted it was overcast with heavy clouds—only a few stars scintillated and then disappeared in the darkening horizon.
>
> Unconsciously I said to myself, "Oh, could this still be our mortal world? How did I get myself into such a strange situation tonight?" Just as I finished muttering these words, I felt as if a piece of soft floss silk were pressing warmly upon my fingers. I took a quick look. Shizuko, who was holding my hand in hers, used the other hand to support herself as she sat down on an aged rock. Thus I stood beside her, unable to let myself go.
>
> (Chap. 16, *MSCC*, III, 98–99)

For fear of falling in love, Saburō decides to cut short his visit with his mother and aunt, to both of whom, as to Shizuko, his abrupt departure will be a serious but unavoidable blow. In a farewell letter to Shizuko, he reveals the secret of his monkhood:

> To my elder sister Shizuko:
>
> Alas! You and I shall never meet again! A Buddhist monk ordained

in the grand precepts of the Law, I can never have the life-long companionship of any woman. But, being neither wood nor stone, how could I not be grateful for your gracious and generous sentiments, your lofty virtue that reaches high to the skies? Born under the ill-omened Water Star, I have encountered in this life unutterable sorrows. How could I have the heart to disturb your tranquillity with the tale of my wanderings and woes? With a monk's staff in my hand, I shall now roam afar as a mendicant. In this dusty world, chances are slim of our seeing each other again. I beg you, elder sister, to let me drag out alone my lingering existence. What else could I do?

Since I am leaving soon in a great hurry, I shall have no time to inform my mother and aunt of the news. My elder sister, please have compassion on me and kindly explain to them the feelings in my heart. Please plead gently with the two elders and ask them not to worry about this perverse child, but to eat well and dress warmly for his sake.

Your younger brother, Saburō,
salutes you in tears.
(Chap. 19, *MSCC*, III, 116–17)

Immediately after writing this letter early in the morning, he has another disquieting encounter with Shizuko before he is able to tear himself away. Finally, when at sea between Nagasaki and Shanghai, he drops Shizuko's embroideries and other mementos into the sea to release himself from the infatuation.

In addition to the love tragedy of Saburō and Shizuko, whose end is not told as is Hsüeh-mei's, there is a minor episode about the unhappy love of a Hunanese monk, Fa-jen, whom Saburō meets at a monastery in Hangchow. Allured by the attentions of a neighboring girl, Fa-jen, then a student, he falls in love with her only to find out that she merely covets his money. She spurns him as soon as he is disinherited by his foster father. Failing to meet her at an appointed time for a rendezvous, he is so afflicted with grief that he attempts suicide by jumping into the water, but he is saved by an old fisherman. In deep despair, he shaves his head to become a monk. He soon becomes Saburō's friend and accompanies him on his journey southward to seek Hsüeh-mei's grave.

In this novel, all minor characters like Fa-jen, Saburō's wet nurse and her son, Saburō's mother, aunt, and sister are only lightly drawn. Even Hsüeh-mei is ill-defined, a part of the background, and a colorless image of virtuous Chinese womanhood. More sprightly and attractive is Shizuko, a refined, intelligent, and lovely young woman. An idealized character, she is endowed with all the intellectual qualities admired by the author; she has an impeccable literary taste, is artistically talented, and possesses a wide knowledge of Chinese painting, poetry, Buddhism, Indian epics, and even Sanskrit grammar! There are, however, other fascinating but non-bluestocking features in her portraiture. Shizuko impresses one with her incomparable beauty, her grace and serenity, her shy and delightfully soft voice, the autumnal gleam of her lustrous eyes, her luxuriant hair, and her light, airy steps. She walks as if wafted by the wind. Although ordinarily modest and retiring, she is sparklingly vivacious, impulsive, and almost bold in her expressions of love for Saburō. The latter takes a rather passive position in their relationship, seemingly resigned to his lot as an ordained monk. It is only in the end that he rises to the occasion, casts aside his vague doubts and timorous desires, and reasserts himself as a man of principle and resolute will who dares precipitate himself into a struggle that ends in tragedy.

The plot unfolds leisurely, and numerous digressions of interest to the author but otherwise unrelated to the main story outline are introduced. Saburō and Shizuko, for instance, several times engage in learned discourses on Chinese poetry and painting. The principals quote poetry, including a translation of Byron's "Ocean," which Saburō completed on the boat from Hong Kong to Yokohama, and an anonymous ballad inscribed on the walls of a picturesque pavilion on West Lake which describes the corrupt practice of purchasing official position. The first seven stanzas of the ballad satirize officeholders of the old bureaucracy. "Unfortunately," the narrator continues, "the last stanza is so badly weather worn by wind and rain as to be indiscernible except for the following couplet:

Heaven having destroyed literature, not even the image of a true writer appears;
With so many shortcuts to officialdom, the scholar shivers in cold despair.

At that time, since the civil service examinations had been abolished, these verses evidently point to returned students from abroad" (Chap. 21, *MSCC*, III, 133).

In spite of its slight characterization and a dilatory plot, *The Lone Swan* captivates the imagination by the intensity of its emotions, its tragic conflict, the novelty of its situation, and the beauty of its language, in which Man-shu achieved a distinct style of his own. As a major Chinese novel of love after *Dream of the Red Chamber*, it succeeds in delineating the conflict between sentiments of love and the inexorable forces of society and religion. Just as family tyranny shapes the destinies of Chia Pao-yü and Lin Tai-yü in the earlier novel, so religion dooms Saburō to his lonely life as a monk. But if Pao-yü is deceived and forced into deserting Tai-yü by the members of his family, Saburō abandons Shizuko of his own volition and in compliance with the Buddhist vow of celibacy. He can very well resolve the conflict by following the dictates of his heart rather than those of his religion, but he has no intention to rebel. It is the desperate but voluntary choice which Saburō makes to "drag out alone his lingering existence" with a broken heart that makes his tragedy more poignant than Pao-yü's. Thus, while *The Lone Swan* lacks the vastness of scope and richness of detail that characterize *Dream of the Red Chamber*, it gains in emotional intensity and singleness of purpose. In addition to its narrative economy, the central love theme is brought into sharper focus by contrast with two minor supporting episodes, Saburō's relationship with Hsüeh-mei and Fa-jen's adventures with the neighboring girl.

Again like *Dream of the Red Chamber*, *The Lone Swan* is generally considered to be an autobiographical novel. Thus it is possible to compare the stories in the novel with the known facts of Man-shu's life, not all of which, however, agree. While critics are divided in their views on this point, there is no denying the fact that Man-shu deliberately cast the novel, admittedly a work of fiction containing more poetry than truth, into autobiographical form, employing real places and personal names, such as Saburō or San-lang, Kawai, Lopez, and Fa-jen. Some Chinese writers even detect a resemblance, rather flimsy it seems, between Shizuko, who plays the zither, and the harpsichord player in Man-shu's poems. There are also correspondences, as indicated earlier, between the novel and the "Postscript to *Voices of the Tide*" in the account of the author's parentage. All this stimulates the curiosity of the reader and gains sympathy for the unfortunate Saburō, especially if the reader happens to believe, in spite of many gaps and inconsistencies, that the stories of Saburō's love for Hsüeh-mei and Shizuko are taken from chapters in the author's own life.

Whether autobiographical or not, Su Man-shu succeeded in creating a make-believe international situation for his novel. While

Japanese by birth and blood, Saburō is typically Chinese in his upbringing, his schooling, his views, and his attitudes. Rather than a split personality, this Sino-Japanese youth is so completely sinicized that he has all the traits of a cultured Chinese whose foreign origin never obtrudes upon the narrative. But no matter how we regard him, Saburō, like Man-shu himself, is above all an international figure whose experiences and activities bridge the two Oriental cultures and cement their relationship through his ties with their respective nationals. Furthermore, rooted in the traditions of the East, Saburō has contacts with the West that are by no means ephemeral or casual. As a student of the Reverend Lopez in Hong Kong, he is well versed in the English language and is capable of appreciating and translating Byron. He is also a friend of Miss Lopez, who presents him with the works of the English poets at their farewell. Later, her correspondence with Saburō arouses in Shizuko suspicions and jealousy that greatly upsets her equanimity on the fateful morning of Saburō's abrupt departure.

To Chinese readers of the early twentieth century, *The Lone Swan* appeared refreshingly new and original when compared with the host of satirical novels on corrupt officialdom and a hypocritical intelligentsia, and the realistic but frivolous novels detailing the lives of sing-song girls in houses of prostitution. The popularity of Man-shu's novel continued throughout the 1920's and 1930's, a time when the literary scene was dominated by authors writing in the vernacular language as a result of the new literature movement initiated by Hu Shih. To be sure, Hu Shih himself had no love for Su Man-shu's stories, which he called "morbidly sexual"—a questionable judgment which will be evaluated in the last chapter of this book—but even the love novels of new writers like Yü Ta-fu and Chang Tzu-p'ing could not compete with *The Lone Swan* in popular acceptance and wide circulation. For very good reasons, George K. Leung, the first translator of modern Chinese fiction into English, chose *The Lone Swan* (1924) as his first attempt in this direction; two years later he completed the English version of Lu Hsün's *True Story of Ah Q* (1926), another landmark of literary accomplishment.

CHAPTER 7

The Journey's End

THE last years of Man-shu's life—from 1912 to 1918—found him plying restlessly across the China Sea between Tokyo and Shanghai, or taking side trips to cities near these two metropolises. An habitual wanderer, Su Man-shu did not complete his restless travels until his final illness. During these six years he found employment only once and very briefly as a teacher at the Anhwei High School in An-ch'ing. Otherwise, he received his sustenance, spiritual as well as material, from his friends in the Southern Society and the China Alliance, reorganized in 1914 into the China Revolutionary party (Chung-hua kê-ming tang). Man-shu's friends not only provided him with outlets for his writings in publications they controlled, although it is doubtful whether he was ever paid for his contributions, but personally furnished funds to help him through difficult days, which were numerous. Nonetheless, he disdained and squandered money whenever a small or large sum came his way. To the very end of his life, he remained poor and received assistance regularly from an ever widening circle of sympathetic friends. Moreover, his friends saw to it that after his death he was given the last rites and a decent burial, and they even erected a monument to perpetuate his memory.

After the close of *The Pacific News*, Man-shu spent the fall of 1912 traveling aimlessly between Japan and Shanghai before he went to An-ch'ing on December 13 to accept a teaching position. Previously, it had been publicly announced that he intended to retranslate Dumas fils's *La Dame aux camélias*, being dissatisfied with Lin Shu's version of the novel for its omissions and errors, but he failed to carry the project through. While in Japan in the same summer, he also attempted to publish a volume of *Sanskrit Vowels and Consonants*, apparently a part of his larger and still unpublished *Sanskrit Grammar*. The new work had been read and its title page inscribed by Kuei Po-hua, a Buddhist follower of Yang Jen-shan and Man-shu's former friend at the Jetavana School, but this publication effort, like several others, came to naught for a lack of funds. Thereafter, it seems, he gave up completely his work on Sanskrit, shifting his time and effort to poetry and fiction. It will be remembered that Man-shu had been encouraged in his Sanskrit studies by Chang Ping-lin and Liu Shih-p'ei, but he was alienated from both men at this time. Liu Shih-p'ei's connection with the Manchu government had segregated him from intellectual circles, while Chang Ping-lin's new political ambitions won little sympathy from his former friend. As late as 1910, Man-shu had addressed a long poem[1] to Chang Ping-lin in response to a poem entitled "The Autumn Night," which Man-shu quoted in the first version of *Random Notes from a Swallow's Mausoleum*. But in a later, revised version of this book, Chang's poem was omitted, and in its place, Man-shu inserted a rather caustic note: "But when I returned to Shanghai [from Java], this retired scholar was visiting the frontier regions with an imperial insignia of office, very much pleased with himself," a reference to Chang Ping-lin's appointment by Yüan Shih-k'ai as pacification commissioner of Manchuria in 1912.

Man-chu's tenure at Anhwei High School in An-ch'ing lasted only half a year, from December, 1912, to the summer of 1913. During this brief sojourn, he renewed old friendships and made new acquaintances with several men of letters. Teng Sheng-hou, a former friend at Wan-chiang School in 1906, was the principal of the school, and Ch'en Tu-hsiu was its dean. Among his colleagues, Man-shu was on intimate terms with Cheng T'ung-sun and Shen Yen-mou. The former, the brother-in-law of Liu Ya-tzu, later became for a number of years a professor at Tsing Hua University, while the latter, after a long career as a business man and an educator, retired to Hong Kong and died only recently. According to Cheng T'ung-sun's testimony, Man-shu, already well known at that time, was besieged by admirers whose visits he tried desperately to avoid. Instead, he preferred the company of Cheng and other friends at a favorite restaurant, The Little Fairyland, where they indulged freely in random discourse on political affairs and past and contemporary personalities. Man-shu was questioned about Sung Chiao-jen, who was then at the height of his fame and influence as a revolutionary leader and a candidate for the premiership of the new Republic. In reply, Man-shu remarked that Sung Chiao-jen was a clever and farsighted person who joined the revolution because he knew that it was bound to be successful sooner or later. Not long afterward, in March, 1913, Sung Chiao-jen was assassinated by agents of Yüan Shih-k'ai. This event led to the Second Revolution, in which Sun Yat-sen's China Revolutionary party was roundly defeated. It also brought about the closure of the high school in An-ch'ing.

The lunar new year and summer vacations of 1913 Man-shu spent with Shen Yen-mou at Cheng T'ung-sun's house in Sheng-chê, a small town near Soochow. At that time Man-shu was engaged in two literary projects: the writing of *Random Notes from a Swallow's Mausoleum* and, together with Shen Yen-mou and Cheng T'ung-sun, a Chinese-English, English-Chinese dictionary. The compilation of the dictionary represented a major undertaking, and it occupied his time for several months. Though the manuscript began to accumulate in disorderly heaps, it was never completed. Only a few fragments survived, and these eventually fell into the hands of Liu Ya-tzu when he set out to collect the literary remains of Su Man-shu. Although Man-shu had started the *Random Notes* earlier in Java, he did not work on them in earnest until this time. The work first appeared serially in November and December, 1913, in the literary supplement of the Shanghai newspaper, *The Daily Life (Sheng-huo jih-pao)*. It was subsequently reprinted four times during the lifetime of the author, with the various versions differing somewhat in wording and the arrangement of the entries, which total sixty-five in their present form. Among extant versions, the one published in Tokyo in the first volume of *The Republic* in May, 1914, may be considered definitive, containing as it does some important revisions of earlier versions.

As a literary genre, "random notes" *(sui-pi)* represent a history of over a thousand years, beginning in the T'ang dynasty. Often anecdotal in nature, such as Man-shu's *Tales of Spectral Splendors on the Shores of Kwangtung*, "random notes" sometimes include "poetry talks" *(shih-hua)*, a form of informal literary criticism initiated by T'ang and Sung writers. The author's *Random Notes from a Swallow's Mausoleum* combines the basic features of both, incorporating in it accounts of personal experiences and observations, as well as remarks on poetry past and present, native and foreign. While couched in the traditional idiom, this volume differs from its prototypes in content and substance, particularly in the exotic elements incorporated in the work. Its interest and novelty, therefore, lies in the author's broad knowledge of Western language and poetry, his background in Sanskrit studies, his monastic experiences, and his life abroad in Japan and Southeast Asia. About twenty items in the latter part of the work, probably jotted down in Surabaya, comment on life and customs in Java, Burma, Ceylon, and India.

While the bulk of the "poetry talks" deal with writings in Chinese, several items are interesting for their insights into the literatures of the East and West:

The ancient poets of India were fond of using the lotus flower[2] as a symbol for their beloved. Similarly, love is symbolized by the Scottish poet [Robert Burns] as a "Red, Red Rose" in a poem of that title, which I translated into a five-word, ancient-style poem in *Voices of the Tide*. (*MSCC*, II, 59)

* * *

The ancient poets in Brahma's land [India] used to say that "a hot hand indicates the seething of a mad passion." There are also these lines in Shakespeare:

"Give me your hand: This hand is moist, my Lady . . . . Hot, hot, and moist." See *Othello*, Act III, Scene 4.

(*MSCC*, II, 60)

* * *

As early spring was fading away and a fine rain drizzled, I opened my volume of Byron's *Poetic Works* and came to the following verse:

To me what is wealth?—it may pass in an hour,

which is the same as Tu Fu's line:

Wealth and rank are to me as the floating clouds.

Byron's lines:

I comprehend, for without transformation,
Men become wolves on any slight occasion . . .

are comparable to T'ao Ch'ien's:

Give my thanks indeed to those young men,
Who behave so meanly to the people they know!
With a hot temper, they destroy wantonly a person's life.
What do I care if I am separated from them?

Byron's lines:

As those who dote on odours pluck the flowers,
And place them on their breast—but place to die—

are similar to those in Li Chia-yu's poem:

When formerly the yellow oriole sang among the flowers,

> *I complained of my life in the green pavilion.*
> *Now, the flowers have fallen and the oriole returns no more—*
> *I too am growing old and your heart is bound to change.*

The last two verses, in which the language is straightforward but the sentiments are deep, similarly affect people in all parts of the world (*MSCC*, II, 43).

In the *Random Notes*, Man-shu wrote on topics that range from the compilation and first printing of the Hebrew Old Testament, or the story of Mohammed's founding of the Islamic religion, to English translations of *Sakuntala* and *Mahabharata*. Of some interest is the following description of the statue of Kama, the god of love in Hindu mythology:

> He holds in his hand a bow of sugarcane, strung with a cluster of bees, and five arrows, each tipped with a love flower, which can pierce the inner heart through the five senses. At the waist hang two hempen sacks filled with odds and ends of incense sticks. His flag is adorned with the picture of a sea monster, which, it is said, the god had subjugated.
>
> (*MSCC*, II, 60–61)

Elsewhere, he reported on the distinction, according to European custom, between a "conventional kiss" and an "emotional kiss" (*MSCC*, II, 42), and repeated the observation of a Western scholar that "Occidentals recognize things through their intellect while Orientals comprehend things through their feelings." *Random Notes* also contains exotic accounts of the six seasons in India, the evil customs of an aboriginal tribe in Burma, the life of a tribal chieftain in Surabaya, and personal experiences at a monastery in the mountains of Central India[3]:

> As the mountains were full of fruit trees, I would pick some fifty to sixty fresh fruits to eat everyday. This continued for almost a month. I was pleased with myself that henceforth I did not have to take any food cooked over fire and smoke. However, I had trouble in moving my bowels, which occurred only once every six days, and I suffered pain each time I did. Later, I contracted dysentery. Only then did I realize that I was far from attaining enlightenment, such opportunity having not yet arrived for me.
>
> (*MSCC*, II, 53)

Man-shu's literary activities in 1913 were not confined to his work on the *Random Notes*. During the same period he wrote a number of poems, including a group of eleven poems entitled "Written in Soochow Using the Rhymes in I-sheng's Poems," and another group of eight poems entitled simply "Without Title." The latter comprise all that was written of the "Three Hundred Poems Without Title" which Man-shu once promised to publish. Reminiscent of the style of the T'ang poet Li Shang-yin, these poems have as their major theme romantic love, sometimes sprinkled with a dash of patriotic sentiment as in the following lines:

The crystal screens are rolled up; dimly a lonely lamp flickers.
Facing the rivers and mountains, silently I pray for our nation's soul.
Even the silver-throated oriole is too timorous to sing,
For fear that its songs will arouse memories of old tear-stains.

Close to the form and spirit of late T'ang poetry with its pretty conceit is the following stanza:

The stars are laid out like a girdle inlaid with gems; the moon is cut like an earring.
All night an autumnal chill screens the bridal chamber.
Even as the wind and dew grow cold on the long embankment,
Withered lotus petals cover a pair of mandarin ducks.

The group of Soochow or Wu poems was actually written in Sheng-chê, as Shen Yen-mou, who is the "I-sheng" in the title, has testified. Furthermore, Shen was understandably embarrassed when friends asked him about his poems, which he did not write. This minor discrepancy aside, the Soochow poems are some of the finest written by Man-shu, and they are quoted here in their entirety:

Written in Soochow, Using the Rhymes in I-sheng's Poems

(1)

The flowers and grasses south of the River are all rooted in grief and gloom,
Yet they provoke the lasses of Wu to frequent laughter and gossip,
As a lonely, heartbroken stranger, riding on a donkey's back,
Passes the city gate in the twilight haze and a drizzling rain.

(2)

Above the blue sea rise peaks of clouds in thousands of layers.
Alas! Where could one entrust oneself all alone in the Middle Kingdom?

Here, in this singing land of Wu, sprinkled with spring mud and fine rain,
I hear again the midnight bell from the Cold Mountain Temple.[4]

(3)

Watery moonbeams drench the steps on the jade terrace;
The incessant sound of tinkling pendants disturbs my dreamy thoughts.
I recall the story that formerly in the palace of Wu,
A hundred flowers bloomed one night in the spring breeze.

(4)

Once, as the setting sun cast aslant its rays on the palace tower,
A jade-green carriage rolled along, driven by precious steeds saddled in gold.
Now that the beautiful one has departed in tears,
The mountains and rivers remain forever forlorn on the edges of this world.

(5)

Where thousands of families were buried in the ashes of calamity,
Stroll the smiling maidens of Wu, as they arrive for a spring outing.
Today, this ancient site has lost the colors of its royal grandeur;
Please do not lead the young deer up the palace tower.

(6)

The river station and the mountain city both look sad and dreary;
Only the withered grass of dreams grows on the Phoenix Terrace.
Spring hues still cherish the site where once there was singing and dancing,
But for whom do these ten thousand flowers thrive in chaotic profusion?

(7)

The blooming years and the rainswept willows have together withered and gone.
Awakened from drink in this corner of the world, I seek the splendors of the Six Dynasties.
Then, suddenly I recall the fair lady, who, under the moonlight,
Once learned to play softly on the flute when no one was around.

(8)

Ten thousand weeping willows waft where the gentle breeze blows,
As I ride westward on my piebald horse east of the paddy fields.
Don't say that the flowering peaches alone display their beauty—
Across the lake on Mount Indigo the setting sun is red.

(9)

On this vast plain the horse neighs mournfully in the twilight:
All alone, a mountain monk chants the song of the Great Summons.[5]
The place where a visitor is afflicted most by grief
Is the Bridge of Willowy Waves by the Rainbow-shaded Pavilion.

(10)

In this azure city of misty trees stands a small red-painted tower,
Where the guest's boat is anchored near the willows in the eastern breeze.
This old country has come to an end in the wake of springtide,
And the people are saddened by the grey partridges crying urgently.

(11)

With white streams and green mountains one's thoughts do not end:
A light mist envelops this human world as well as the skies above.
In the Red-Clay Temple, as the wind gently wafts and the rain drizzles,
One sees not the returning monk but only the homecoming swallows.

One should add here that although Man-shu did not write these poems in Soochow, he did visit this historical city several times on the way from Shanghai to Sheng-chê. Once he spent almost a month there in the home of Cheng T'ung-sun's elder brother, where he and his friends continued their work on the dictionary. It may also be mentioned that this lonely, heartbroken, donkey-riding traveler, while passing the city gate of Soochow in the gloaming drizzle, fell from the donkey's back and, as he reported the incident jocularly to Liu Ya-tzu, "almost became a limping immortal."

It was at this time also that Man-shu passed the hours whenever he was in Shanghai in "feasts of wine and flowers." "Flowers," symbolic of loveliness and tenderness, refer to sing-song girls, who have been the "Muses" of Chinese literature since the T'ang period. They are celebrated in T'ang dynasty poetry, as in Yüan drama and Ch'ing fiction, which often feature stories of sing-song girls. They should not be confused, therefore, with the common run of prostitutes. Beautiful and seductive, these women were trained in the arts, and many were well versed in instrumental and vocal music, dance, painting, chess, and poetry. Nonetheless, such talents grew rarer as the times went by. Thus, although most of these girls in early twentieth-century China could still sing and play musical instruments, they were not known for their skill in dancing like the geishas in Japan. In Shanghai, they established themselves in the pleasure quarters in the International Settlement along Hankow and Foochow roads, where a multitude of restaurants and teahouses were also located. During the feast, each guest could summon a "flower" to keep him company. She would adorn his table and urge him to drink in the course of a prolonged dinner. While most of these girls were at the beck and call of wealthy patrons, some did "go steady" with male patrons, and a romance could develop in this way.

Su Man-shu began to attend "feasts of wine and flowers" in the fall of 1907, when he was staying at the association library with Ch'en Ch'ü-ping, Huang Chieh, and other members of the Association for the Preservation of National Learning. But it was during the years 1912–13 that he regularly kept the company of a bevy of "flower" girls, a list of whose "fragrant" names and addresses he kept in his diary. Though still known among his friends as "Monk Su," he thus indulged himself in non-Buddhist pleasures and all but discarded his religious burdens, except the cassock and his Buddhist certificate which he kept until his death. This does not mean, however, that he transgressed his vow of chastity or that he went much beyond lighthearted sentimental attachments. He merely allowed himself the privilege of catching up with the fashions of the times, of indulging in games which his friends, whether they were conservators of national learning or revolutionaries of the Southern Society, were accustomed to playing. For these intellectuals, the period immediately preceding and following the Second Revolution was one of trial and tribulation, and many were not loathe to seek moments of delectation and dissipation. Still, one reads in wonderment the expense account kept in his diary, which records lavish expenditures on such parties, sometimes amounting to several hundred dollars.

The sing-song girls, however, also provided a source of consolation when they twice visited him on his sickbed in 1912 and 1913. In a letter dated December 4, 1912, Man-shu wrote to a friend in Hong Kong: "Recently I was laid up in the hotel by a slight indisposition. All my friends having been isolated from me, only a few female 'book collators' [a euphemism for high-class courtesans] came to visit. I never expected that feelings of good friendship would still be cherished by anyone from the ranks of fallen leaves and drifting flowers." The next year, he noted rather factually in his diary: "On the 17th day of the 10th month, in the cyclical year Kuei-ch'ou [November 14, 1913], at two o'clock in the afternoon, Chou Wu, Hsüeh San, T'ung-hua, and Tai-yün came to visit and comfort me at my sickbed. I kept silent without uttering one word." According to the same diary, it was on Chou Wu that Man-shu spent $75, and on Hsüeh San, $356.

During his stay in Shanghai in 1913, Man-shu made his headquarters at the Number One Hotel on Nanking Road in the International Settlement. One of the episodes at that time he recorded in his *Random Notes from a Swallow's Mausoleum*:

> On one occasion, Chang Chüan-chüan [Chang, the Graceful Maiden] wrote down at a dinner party the following four-line poem:
>
> *This gentlemen, Vimalakirti, is too raving mad;*
> *Whence come these Heavenly Maidens with a shower of sweet fragrance?*
> *I laugh at myself for having a Buddhist heart that is as dry as a log,*
> *So no harm will be done even if I keep the company of a flowering sprig.*
>
> Chüan-chüan told me that the poem was composed by the monk, Ching-an. I said, "The monk wrote these verses on the spur of a gleeful moment. He was not aping the needle-swallowing Raksha" (*MSCC*, II, 40).

In addition to Chang Chüan-chüan, his favorite sing-song girl in Shanghai was Hua Hsüeh-nan (Flower Snow-south), whom he first met in 1907. Born in the Chinese community in Singapore, Hua Hsüeh-nan drifted to Shanghai in her teens, where she became widely known. On these two "flower" girls, Man-shu commented: "Hua Hsüeh-nan has a wintry air, whereas Chang Chüan-chüan has an autumnal breath"—Chang being somewhat serious and somber and Hua no longer young and sprightly.

The following story was told by Liu Ya-tzu: "In the first month of the lunar calendar, 1913, I went to Shanghai and learned that Man-shu was still there. One evening [March 20], he invited me to a wine-and-flower party at Hua Hsüeh-nan's house. Among the guests were Chu Shao-p'ing, Yeh Ch'u-ts'ang, and also Ch'en Ying-shih [Ch'en Ch'i-mei]. Before he had finished his dinner, Ying-shih left in a great hurry, saying that he had to go to the railway station to send off Sung Chiao-jen, who was leaving on a mission to North China. Who would have expected that the paper the next morning would report the news of Sung Chiao-jen's assassination on that very night? Thus the policy of the Right-wing Nationalists to use Yüan Shih-k'ai to settle the political problems of the time failed completely. Thereafter, the situation in China underwent a drastic change" (*MSCC*, V, 185).

The situation reached its climax when the Nationalists fled in large numbers to Japan after their defeat by Yüan Shih-k'ai in the Second Revolution. Man-shu, who had written a manifesto for the anti-Yüan campaign, also went to Japan in December, 1913, expressly for the treatment of a chronic intestinal ailment. He announced his departure from Shanghai in a letter to Liu Ya-tzu: "How sorry I was not able to see you before I left! Sickness again seized me soon after I got to Kyoto. It's hard to figure out, Ya-tzu, whether I shall have again the pleasure of holding your hands! The rivers and mountains are indeed beautiful but they merely increase one's sorrows" (*MSCC*, I, 278). Man-shu's health, which had never been strong, worsened. Three times within the first month in Japan he was afflicted by illness, the last time by malaria. During a period of recuperation, he complained that he could only take bread and milk, but was pleased later that he could eat three bowls of thin rice with beef, eggs, and pickled preserves from Nara. His greatest complaint, however, was that the doctors forbade him to smoke cigars and that the medicine, which he had to take three times a day, was extremely bitter. "How could medicine," he moaned, "taste as palatably as 'eight-precious' rice pudding?" Then came the New Year season, and against doctor's order he feasted himself on indigestible, glutinous rice cakes at the homes of friends and relatives until he suffered the unhappy consequences of his own reckless action.

When not plagued by sickness, Man-shu took trips to scenic spots near Tokyo and Kyoto and along the seacoast. He became interested in the teachings of the *San-lun* (Japanese *Sanron*) or Madhyamika sect of Buddhism, but generally he seemed to take religion as well as life in an overtly lighthearted vein, as shown in the following excerpts from letters to friends:

> I got dysentery yesterday but am slightly better this morning. Henceforth, I shall devote myself to the study of Buddhism so that Brahma will protect me in my future life! (To Hsü Jen-ju, August 19, 1914)

> I sat quietly the whole day, knowing full well in my heart that I did it

not for meditation but because of illness. (To Shao Yüan-ch'ung, September 7, 1914)

After the end of the war in Europe, I would like to take a trip to the West to visit Byron's grave. . . . As for the affairs of our country, we can only leave them in Buddha's hands as there is little else that we can do. Please tell me of any adventures you may have had. (To Teng Meng-shih, October 8, 1914)

What are you doing in New York? I trust you are not going to be infatuated by those doting sirens. (To Teng Meng-shih, January 5, 1915)

The last two passages are taken from Man-shu's letters to Teng Meng-shih, a member of the revolutionary group who had left Tokyo in mid-1914 to study at Columbia University. In another letter to the same friend (December 30, 1914), he wrote in a jocular vein.

But I would advise you against consuming too much milk and beef. Don't you see that the young people of today are so fond of dairy products that they have acquired a bovine temperament, which one should guard oneself against? But if you insist that you cannot swallow your bread without milk or beef, then you should go to a grocery store in Chinatown to buy some fermented soybean cheese of the best grade; you can spend ten dollars for the red colored brand and another ten dollars for the white. Then spread it on the bread, eat it slowly, and you will find it tastes just heavenly. If your landlord should ask you what it is, you can tell him that the red kind is red-rose cheese and the white kind, white-rose cheese, and he will shake his head in amazement at such Chinese delicacies! (*MSCC*, I, 304–5)

While in Japan, Man-shu formed a close friendship with Teng Meng-shih (before Teng left for the United States), as well as with several other prominent members of the China Revolutionary Party such as Chü Cheng, Shao Yüan-ch'ung, T'ien T'ung, and Tai Chi-t'ao, all of whom were leading a life of exile there. He was also introduced to their leader, Sun Yat-sen, a fellow Hsiang-shanese, but it is doubtful whether Man-shu ever became a member of the party. However, when *The Republic*, the party organ, was first published in May, 1914, Man-shu contributed three items: a collection of sixteen poems; a new version of his *Random Notes from a Swallow's Mausoleum*; and his second novel, *Red Tears at the End of the World.* Unfortunately, only two chapters of this last work were published, as Man-shu failed to complete the story. In the extant portion there is little indication of plot and no explanation of the meaning of the title. It seems to have been intended as a romantic story interwoven with love, chivalry, and revenge, set in a time of war and warlord tyranny. Among the important characters who appear in the first few pages are the hero, a handsome, upright young man of chivalric nature; an old, retired swordsman leading the life of a hermit in a beautiful secluded spot with his young, charming, and cultured daughter, who is also an expert in swordsmanship; and the old man's brother, a fortuneteller of high intelligence and distinguished bearing. The story also involves a married woman whom the student previously rescued from danger and misery. Thus the stage is set, the characters are introduced in their respective roles, but the drama is never enacted. No reason is indicated for the termination of the novel. In such a fragmentary state, the work is negligible.

After only six issues, all published in 1914, *The Republic* ceased publication when its contributors scattered to all parts of the world. Some, like Teng Meng-shih, went abroad to pursue advanced studies, and others traveled to China and Southeast Asia in preparation for a third revolution. Man-shu, however, continued his stay in Japan and remained an outsider from political activities. Instead, he engaged himself in literary work, which produced a group of "Nineteen Miscellaneous Poems Written during My Sojourn in Japan," fifteen of which first appeared in *The Republic.* These contain tender and romantic sentiments typical of him, but they show a firmer grasp of the rules of versification for the seven-word, four-line form *(ch'i-chüeh)*, which for him was his chief mode of expression. As they are not much different in nature and content from his earlier works, only a few examples will suffice:

(2)

The flitting glowworm gleams and dims—long, long is the night;
The Chaste Maiden,[6] fair and debonair, finds autumn unbearable.
Please do not ask me, when we meet, about affairs in this mortal world.
The old country so grieves my heart that only tears flow.

(5)

Don't pilfer like a prodigal this famed fragrance of a foreign land!
Her smiles through the window screen make my thoughts unduly gloomy.

I would like to present her with a lustrous pearl, but I despair and falter,
For fear it will kindle sorrows anew when next year the twin stars meet.

(7)

The swing in the deep courtyard, the moon hanging like a hook—
In love with the flower shadows, she loathes to mount the stairs.
Her stockings are soaked by the dew under an undulation of blooming red lotuses,
As she fondles her silken girdle, putting to shame the pale maiden in the moon.

In 1914, Man-shu published his third anthology of Chinese and English poetry, the first two being *Affinities in Literature* (1908) and *Voices of the Tide* (1911). Entitled *Esoteric Essences of Chinese and English Poetry*, it differs from the two previous volumes in that it is devoted almost entirely to English translations of Chinese poems, none of which are by Man-shu himself. Like its predecessors, the book contains selections from the *Poetry Classic*, the ancient style poetry of the Han and earlier periods, the works of T'ao Ch'ien and others of the Six Dynasties period, and T'ang poetry, chiefly by Li Po and Tu Fu. Some of these translations had been previously announced for the second volume of *Affinities in Literature*, which never saw publication. This volume contains also a translation of Li Ling's famous letter to his friend Su Wu, in which the Han general, who had surrendered to the Huns, spiritedly defends his position as a defector, as well as a prose passage on "true form" from one of the treatises in the *Mahayana*. Lacking any of his own compositions, or reproductions of his paintings and photographs, *Esoteric Essences of Chinese and English Poetry* is important only as another example of his interest in East-West literary relations.

His residence in Japan from December, 1913, to May, 1916, was his longest stay there since the five years of schooling (1898–1903) at Ta-t'ung and Waseda. Between traveling extensively in the country and lying sick in the hospital, he spent nearly two and a half years in Tokyo, at one time living with Chü Cheng, editor of *The Republic*. Presumably, he must have seen Kawai fairly often, although there is no mention in his letters of visits with her. Literary activities, as we have seen, occupied a great deal of his time. After the demise of *The Republic* in late 1914, Man-shu found another outlet for his writings in *The Tiger (Chia-yen tsa-chih)*, a monthly publication edited by Chang Shih-chao, his friend at the time of the *National*

People's Daily (1903). Early numbers of *The Tiger*, first issued in June, 1914, in Tokyo, make several references to Man-shu, mostly in the form of poems by his friends. In the same year appeared his preface to Chang Shih-chao's "A Tale of Twin Chessboards," which narrates the love and suicide through drowning of their friend, Ho Mei-shih. Another common friend, Ch'en Tu-hsiu, also contributed a preface to the tale. Further evidence of the literary affinities of the three men can be found in the prefaces which Chang Shih-chao and Ch'en Tu-hsiu wrote in turn for Man-shu's "A Tale of Crimson Silk," which appeared in the seventh issue of *The Tiger* in July, 1915. By that time, Chang Shih-chao had moved *The Tiger* to Shanghai, where Ch'en Tu-hsiu also joined him, but Man-shu continued his stay in Japan throughout 1915.

His first attempt at short-story writing, "A Tale of Crimson Silk," is as weak in structure as it is precipitate in action, the scene shifting continuously from one place to another. There is little plot development or characterization, as in *The Lone Swan*, and the story itself is overcrowded with a host of episodes that deal with as many as four pairs of young lovers: (1) T'an-luan, the first-person narrator, and Mai Wu-ku (the Fifth Maiden); (2) Hsüeh Meng-chu, who becomes a Buddhist monk in Soochow, and Hsieh Ch'iu-yün; (3) Lo Fei-yü, an English teacher in Shanghai, and Emma Lu, a flirt; (4) Yü-luan, a girl educated in England, and her fiancé, a wastrel. Adequate treatment is given the main story of T'an-luan and Wu-ku, which interweaves rather loosely with the secondary story of Hsüeh Meng-chu (quasi-homophonous with Su Man-shu) and Ch'iu-yün, the other two episodes being merely mentioned in passing.

In spite of these weaknesses, "A Tale of Crimson Silk" is notable for its theme of supreme love, at whose altar all the major characters, except the flirt and the wastrel, sacrifice themselves, either carrying their wounds with them into the realm of Buddhist emptiness like T'an-luan, Ch'iu-yün, and Yü-luan, or suffering death from sickness (Mai Wu-ku), suicide (Lo Fei-yü), and transformation, in the Buddhist manner, into ashes (Hsüeh Meng-chu). In the last instance, the scene of Meng-chu's death is described rather vividly by T'an-luan, the narrator, as follows:

> Soon, in early spring, I accompanied Ch'iu-yün to Shanghai to look for Meng-chu. When we got to Soochow, a girl student from a missionary

school told Ch'iu-yün: "All the people in Soochow know about this monk, Meng-chu, who lives on sweets every day. Recently, he moved to a small temple, called Immeasurable, outside the city."

Immediately, I went with Ch'iu-yün to seek him. When we got there, the pine shadows covered the front gate, it being the night of the full moon. I noticed that the door was ajar, so I asked Ch'iu-yün to wait outside as I entered the temple. Inside, the courtyard was empty, the night still, and only the light of Buddha's lamp flickered on the four walls. I continued forward to a side room, which was also quiet and vacant. Thinking that Meng-chu had not yet returned, I retraced my steps until I caught a glimpse of a white-faced idol at a corner of the courtyard corridor. As I approached, I saw that it was Meng-chu himself, sitting there lifeless with eyes closed and grass growing between his knees. I called him, but got no reply. I pulled at his hand and it was as stiff as iron. Only then did I realize that Meng-chu had died a Buddhist death.

I hurried out to tell Ch'iu-yün. She entered and stood silently in front of him, without uttering one word. All of a sudden, she saw a corner of a crimson silk kerchief[7] protruding from the lapel of his cassock. She pulled it out with her hand, looked around, and turned it over. Then she nestled herself in Meng-chu's lap as she embraced and kissed him with streaming tears. All this time I stood still. Suddenly, I heard the rustling of the wind as Meng-chu's corpse dissolved into ashes, only the piece of crimson silk remaining in Ch'iu-yün's hand. She then wrapped some ashes in her kerchief and placed it inside her dress. At that time, the wind continued to blow until all the ashes were dispersed, leaving only Ch'iu-yün and myself in the temple. (*MSCC*, III, 219–20)

The idea of supreme love which finds its consummation in death is praised by Ch'en Tu-hsiu and Chang Shih-chao in their prefaces to this story. Both mention Oscar Wilde as an outstanding writer and the one who gave this subject its finest expression in *Salomé* and *The Picture of Dorian Gray*. Apropos of Wilde's novel, Chang Shih-chao wrote: "When I read it, I couldn't help from commenting with a sigh that it is the actress (who plays Juliet in Shakespeare's play) who truly understands life. Since she already knows the truth about life, there is nothing to prevent her from death if she fails to attain it, no matter in what kind of environment she finds herself. For the same reason my friend Ho Mei-shih died; also for this reason Hsüeh Meng-chu, T'an-luan's friend, suffered a Buddhist transformation and Lo Fei-yü committed suicide. Well indeed has T'uan-luan said, 'They all die for true love' " (*MSCC*, IV, 44–45). For Ch'en Tu-hsiu, the significance of the story derives from the fact that "T'an-luan survives while Wu-ku dies; Meng-chu passes away while Ch'iu-yün lives on. Whatever the denouement, be it death or survival, each exerts his or her utmost in a desperate assault on love and death. Yet, when Wu-ku is about to die, she holds out the promise of meeting T'an-luan in their afterlife. When Meng-chu who had just been enlightened on matters of life and death and who should be completely emancipated from any lingering doubts and affection died, there still appeared in his ashes a corner of the crimson silk kerchief. Whether in love or death, what matters after all is the way of its consummation" (*MSCC*, IV, 47). The comments of these two writers show how they and Man-shu regarded and evaluated this story—not from the technical viewpoint of its construction and characterization, but from the human aspect of love and death, the significance of which Man-shu attempted to illustrate through a multiplicity of personalities and relationships that afford comparison and contrast. One must conclude, therefore, that Man-shu succeeded in achieving a semblance of unity in the theme of this story, in spite of its rambling and loosely connected episodes.

Immediately following the completion of "A Tale of Crimson Silk," Man-shu published in the August, 1915, issue of *The Tiger* "A Tale on the Burning of the Sword." The latter is a fast-moving story of adventure, replete with bizarre situations and caustic satire. Although it contains a love story of Tu-ku Ts'an, a chivalrous young man, and Liu A-lan, a typically beautiful, tender, devoted girl, the plot revolves mainly around the unfortunate lives of a number of young people, including the hero and the heroine, amidst an inhumane society in a war-ridden land. It is a time of great turmoil in the country, when the people suffer from hunger, flood, and death at the hands of rebellious soldiers. Entrusted by a dying old hermit with the care of his two charming granddaughters, A-lan and her younger sister, Tu-ku Ts'an leads them to safety in Hong Kong, but not without experiencing some harrowing experiences. Once they have to hide themselves for several nights in a "ghost village," where the inhabitants have all been slaughtered by the soldiery. Finally Tu-ku Ts'an leaves the girls at the home of their aunt in Hong Kong, while he continues alone on his journey after having received a pledge of love from A-lan.

Young and pretty, A-lan soon becomes the target of a matrimonial maneuver by her aunt and has to flee from home to seek her own destiny. She experiences a similar mishap in the house of a wealthy family, to which she has hired herself as a maidservant. In her aimless wanderings she picks up a companion, Mei-niang, who is about to leap into the water to escape the clutches of a cruel stepmother. Disguising themselves as beggars, the two travel together under trying circumstances. Once, they meet on the road a "man-eating" general, "who looked like a returned student from abroad." Later they stay at an inn kept by an old couple, who turn out to be cannibals. The girls make their way out of the inn just as the old man is sharpening a butcher's knife in anticipation of a delicious repast. In their flight, they cross the flooded countryside by riding on a broken drum. Exhausted and suddenly taken ill, A-lan dies on the way, three times calling out Tu-ku's name in her dying moments. The story does not end with the death of the heroine, however, but continues with Mei-niang's struggles for survival until she finally settles down contentedly as the wife of an opium-den owner! In the meantime, Tu-ku Ts'an had succeeded in avenging his friend's death by cutting off the murderer's ears with his sword. His mission accomplished, he burns the sword as if it were a piece of paper and then disappears from this world without a trace.

The "Tale on the Burning of the Sword" is therefore a nominal tale of love. While well written in its early parts, it dwindles in interest as the story goes along and devolves into a string of incidents that are grotesque, revolting, and grossly exaggerated. The only unifying theme in this tale is its panoramic presentation of the chaotic and miserable conditions of the times, which deeply affect the lives of the hapless women of the story. It also serves as a vehicle for the author's denunciation, through the mouths of these unfortunates, of human foibles and social tyrannies. When on the verge of being forced to marry a man employed as a second-class secretary in a foreign-owned pastry shop (he has just returned from abroad with a PhD from the "Dollar Country"), A-lan says with a long sigh: "People all regard me as mere chattel to be traded. How my heart jumps and my face burns with shame! I just have to run away from this disgrace" (*MSCC*, III, 236). On an earlier and happier occasion, her younger sister asks innocently but critically, "What is the use of studying in such a turbulent and devastating world? Scholars who are conversant with current affairs merely talk loudly and idly in order to obtain fame and wealth. As for those crafty politicians and specious talkers, they harm the people with their ambitions and contrivances" (*MSCC*, III, 227). In another episode, the workings of Heaven are questioned by a living "corpse," whom Tu-ku Ts'an and the two sisters encounter in the "ghost village." Just revived from death, the man recounts to them the massacre of his fellow villagers by the soldiery: "Although the people here were of low and humble origin, they nevertheless tilled the land for their food and wove their own clothing. None of them ever acted unlawfully. And yet, how Heaven sports with human life!" (*MSCC*, III, 231).

Man-shu continued to devote his energies to story-writing when he returned to China in 1916. He had given up poetry, it seems, since the publication of his "Miscellaneous Poems Written during My Sojourn in Japan." Probably he found little inspiration for poetry in the remaining years of his life, beset as they were by chronic illness and the threat of death. Personal letters to his Southern Society friends like Liu Ya-tzu and Ts'ai Shou became less frequent, shorter, and more factual, lacking the spark of intellect and emotion that make his earlier letters to Liu San and Kao T'ien-mei so engrossing. On the other hand, his last few letters read like the lingering gasps of a tired and sick man, which he was, complaining of nervous tension, neurasthenia, chest pains, piles, dysentery, and intestinal and stomach disorders.

Only once in the last years of his life did Man-shu have an occasion for excitement. In May, 1916, news reached him of a military coup by Shantung revolutionary forces, led by Chü Cheng and Shao Yüan-ch'ung, against the reactionary regime of Yüan Shih-k'ai. Still in Japan at the time, he was so overjoyed that he immediately set out for Tsingtao, Shantung, to visit his friends. After repeated failures in previous years, the China Revolutionary party under the leadership of Sun Yat-sen had finally completed arrangements in early 1916 for another military compaign against Yüan Shih-k'ai. Among Man-shu's friends of *The Republic* period, T'ien T'ung was appointed military governor of Hupeh; Chü Cheng, commander in chief of the Northeastern Army in charge of Chihli (Hopei), Shantung, and Shansi; Shao Yüan-ch'ung, garrison commander of Tsingtao. Accompanied by Tai Chi-t'ao, Sun Yat-sen himself had gone to Shanghai to direct the new revolution. A rapid succession of events followed in the next few months. On May 18, the revolutionists suffered a setback when Ch'en Ch'i-mei, like Sung Chiao-jen, was assassinated by Yüan's agents in Shanghai, but they found cause for celebration when Yüan Shih-k'ai, his ambition to become emperor frustrated by a military uprising in

Yunnan, died on June 6, thus bringing the impending civil war to an end. With peace restored, Man-shu was able to spend his days in Tsingtao in a relaxed and casual atmosphere, visiting scenic Mount Lao in the outskirts of this beautiful seaport and playing mah-jongg with the ladies in Chü Cheng's residence. According to a friend who was with him at the time, his health had so deteriorated that he no longer enjoyed mountain climbing even when carried in a sedan-chair. He also proved to be a poor gambler, although the jingling sounds of mah-jongg tiles generally raised his spirits.

Returning to Shanghai, Man-shu stayed for a short while at Sun Yat-sen's residence on the Rue Vallon in the French Concession. In November and December, he visited Hangchow before returning to Shanghai for the New Year's celebrations. In the meantime, his third short story was published in the November and December issues of *La Jeunesse (Hsin ch'ing-nien tsa-chih)*, a magazine also known as *The New Youth*, edited by Ch'en Tu-hsiu. Regarding this story, "Tale of a Broken Hairpin," Ch'en Tu-hsiu wrote in a postscript:

> I always feel that there must be a reason for everything, whether good or bad, that happens in this world. It also holds true for ordinary daily events—as there is no reason why they should not happen. It is human nature to seek food and beauty, not to mention a lifelong mate for whom one cherishes a deep affection. But before man can get out of this dark and savage world, the oppressions of evil social customs weigh heavily upon his individual will. While their baneful effect is not limited to this single aspect, the loss of freedom of action is the most painful. All works of fiction, past and present, Chinese and foreign, were written to uphold this thesis. Formerly, when my friends Man-shu and Ch'u-t'ung [Chang Shih-chao] wrote respectively "A Tale of Crimson Silk" and "A Tale of Twin Chessboards," they both expressed the same idea and to each of these stories I wrote a preface. Now, Man-shu again asks me to introduce his "Tale of a Broken Hairpin," and still I take the same view. I wonder whether the author will laugh at me for being so farfetched in my interpretation of his purpose. (*MSCC*, IV, 49)

Employing the timeworn theme of triangular love, Man-shu succeeded nonetheless in presenting in "Tale of a Broken Hairpin" a moving account of a love affair between Chuang Chih, a friend of the narrator Man-shu, and two lovely girls, Ling-fang and Lien-p'ei. Equally charming, refined, and talented, the two girls are both deeply in love with Chuang Chih, whose attractions, however, are not clearly spelled out in the narrative. Perhaps, it is because he has a genuine personality and a kind heart. He loves Ling-fang tenderly. Nevertheless, he can be cold and distant, as when he repels Lien-p'ei's advances. This he does under great emotional strain, as Lien-p'ei is virtually irresistible, and is, moreover, the choice of his uncle and aunt, to whom he owes his upbringing. Thus, a conflict develops which Chuang Chih cannot resolve. While he is bewildered to the point of inaction, forces already set in motion cannot be stopped until all three are plunged into the abyss of tragedy.

While Chuang Chih lies ill in the hospital, he is visited by Ling-fang, who gives him her jade hairpin as a token of her love. "Should Heaven thwart human desires," she states, "let it break into pieces!" After Chuang Chih leaves the hospital, he goes with Man-shu to live with his uncle and aunt in the Shanghai suburbs. Lien-p'ei comes for a visit, and on her birthday they go out for a grand tour of the city, accompanied by Chuang Chih's aunt and Man-shu. They spend the day driving and shopping, the evening at an opera, and the night in a Western-style hotel. Returning home the next morning, Chuang Chih finds the hairpin, which he had hidden under his pillow, broken. During his absence, Ling-fang had come to visit him and was received by his uncle; after having persuaded Ling-fang to give up Chuang Chih, the uncle broke the hairpin at her bidding. Following this inauspicious event, the story rapidly reaches a climax with the death of all three major participants. Lien-p'ei cuts her throat in despair at Chuang Chih's rejection of her love; Ling-fang hangs herself after the fateful encounter with Chuang Chih's uncle; brokenhearted, Chuang Chih also passes away.

The longest and the best of his short stories, "Tale of a Broken Hairpin" describes vividly and in some detail the interrelationships and personal reactions of three sensitive and hapless young lovers entrapped in the web of unrelenting fate. To a Western reader, their precipitous plunge to death may appear to be insufficiently motivated, but against the background of a tyrannical social tradition, many persons, unprepared for the rough-and-tumble struggle of life, did take their own lives when they failed to extricate themselves from unresolvable social conflicts. Thus Ch'en Tu-hsiu saw fit to blame the tragedy, for lack of a real villain, on the reactionary forces of society that deny free expression of human will or the assertion of individuality. The author's own explanation of the tragedy is rather startling. "All women under Heaven," he wrote, "are sources of calamity." That issue aside, the story does excel in drama and pathos. In writing this moving tale of love, Man-shu was in his element. Uncluttered by lengthy digressions and unburdened by a plethora of morbid sentiment and incident, "Tale of a Broken Hairpin" reflects subtle characterization and a well-designed plot. An improvement over his own earlier stories as well as those by his contemporaries, it represents a new maturity in the art of fiction writing, though not in his emotional life or wordly wisdom. He never in fact attained full emotional maturity as a man.

Unlike the swiftly moving scene in his short story, the last days of his own life passed without memorable incident. The first half of 1917 found him traveling between Shanghai and Japan, where he paid Kawai what turned out to be his last visit. He was taken ill in early summer when in Shanghai. During the second half of the year he moved from one hospital to another, staying occasionally with friends. At one time, he was a guest in the apartment of Chiang Kai-shek in the International Settlement.[8] "In the summer of 1917, Mr. Chiang Kai-shek told me," wrote Ch'en Kuo-fu, the nephew of Ch'en Ch'i-mei and a former student at the Ch'ang-sha school where Su Man-shu taught briefly, "that Mr. Su was sick in Shanghai at a hospital in Rue Joffre and asked me to send him some money. For this reason, I had another chance to visit him. I found he had stomach trouble and had been suffering a great deal in the hospital. So Mr. Chiang invited him to come to live with us at No.11, Hsin-min Lane" (*MSCC*, IV, 351). In the same winter, Man-shu became so ill that he had to be moved to Hai-ning Hospital on Pao-ch'ang Road. At the same time, he was also in great financial trouble. Once, when a friend visited him, he produced a batch of pawnshop tickets for his friend to redeem. When another friend went to see him, Man-shu held his hand and said, "I don't have a watch with me. I feel dizzy day and night. When my life comes to an end, I will not know what hour of the day it will be" (*MSCC*, V, 251). His friend took off his wristwatch and gave it to him. Then he was asked to see the director of the hospital to complain about its neglect of the patient. In reply, the doctor showed the friend three or four packages of roasted chestnuts which he had confiscated from beside Man-shu's pillow. Thus his illness dragged on to the first months of 1918.

Plagued by illness, Man-shu's only contribution in 1917[9] was "The Tale That Was No Dream," which was published in the December, 1917, issue of *The Grand Magazine (Hsiao-shuo ta-kuan)*, edited by Pao T'ien-hsiao, a friend of the Soochow school period and a well-known writer in Shanghai literary circles at the time. Man-shu's last story is a variation on the theme of the eternal triangle, which he had presented successfully in the earlier story, "Tale of a Broken Hairpin." Unfortunately, "The Tale That Was No Dream" is an inferior work. The dramatic interest centers around Hai-ch'in, a typical young student, and Wei-hsiang and Feng-hsien, two fair rivals for his affection, but the story is marred by a series of coincidences and improbabilities. There are also some minor sensual descriptions, particularly of Feng-hsien's aggressive but futile effort to seduce Hai-ch'in. In Man-shu's stories, women always take the initiative in such instances, but these passages are milder in this respect than fiction typical of the time and should not be construed as obscene or immoral in any sense. A gentle and weak young man, Hai-ch'in rebels against harsh authority, personified by his aunt, and escapes worldly entanglements through the gate of Buddhism. Feng-hsien, a loser in the game of love, lives through her disappointment. But she gains little sympathy from the reader because of flaws in her character. She is forward and fond of intrigue and deception, all geared to a desperate attempt to catch the elusive male animal. The heroine of the story, Wei-hsiang, a paragon of feminine virtue, is doomed by a conspiracy of events to imprisonment and eventually to suicide by drowning. There is no beautiful dream in "The Tale That Was No Dream," but the following remark by Hai-ch'in may serve to explain the meaning of the title: "People of this world can easily find in dream-land a genuine sense of exhilaration, whereas in broad daylight even the wide sea and the vast skies become dreary and uninspiring" (*MSCC*, III, 308).

This spirit of exhilaration, certainly, Man-shu never regained. The best he could do was to cling to the hopes of recovery given him by doctors in his more comfortable days, which were few and far between. Occasionally, he expressed, as in a letter to Liu Ya-tzu in March, 1918, the hope of visiting friends after he left the hospital. By that time, he had already moved from Hai-ning to Kuang-tz'u Hospital on Rue Pere Robert in the French Concession. While at Kuang-tz'u, Man-shu stayed in a room next to Chü Cheng. One day when the same friend who had given him the watch came to visit, the visitor and Chü Cheng, to put Man-shu in a good humor, told him that they had had a vision in which Buddha had appeared in the clouds and announced that Man-shu would soon recover from his illness. Blessed by this revelation, he joined his hands in a gesture of devotion and gave his thanks to the great divinity. But this kind of optimism did not last long, and even the promise of divine help came to naught when death struck him on May 2, 1918. In his dying moments, Man-shu expressed concern for his aged mother in Japan. Finally, he said, "Love embraces all; as for impediments, there are none."

When his friends made an inventory of his belongings in the hospital, they found little else but rouge boxes and perfume sachets. A handwritten copy of Man-shu's miscellaneous notes and diaries, mostly income and expenditure accounts, came into the possession of Hsiao Jen-ch'iu, a friend from *The Republic* period in Japan. Other manuscripts, including one in a strange form of writing, which was probably the *Sanskrit Grammar*, were said to have been in Kawai's keeping at her house in Yokohama. All of these manuscripts were destroyed during the great earthquake of September, 1923.

On May, 1918, there appeared in *The Republican Daily (Min-kuo jih-pao)*, a Shanghai newspaper and the organ of the China Revolutionary party edited by Yeh Ch'u-ts'ang, the following "Obituary of the Reverend Man-shu":

> The Reverend Man-shu, Su Hsüan-ying, was well-versed in prose and poetry, and skillful in painting. Thus he was able to channel into his works the interrelationships and mutual influences of the arts and literatures of the East and West. He had an especially exalted moral character. Lately, distressed by the decadence of society and the confusion of the national political situation, he planned to visit Rome to investigate the arts in that great metropolis, but he was prevented from making the trip because of frequent sickness. Last April, he was afflicted by a serious stomach ailment and he lingered for a long time on the sick bed. He went to several hospitals for treatment. Occasionally, his condition improved, but before long it took a serious turn. Thus, at four o'clock yesterday afternoon he finally passed away at Kuang-tz'u Hospital. Funeral arrangements have been made by Mr. Wang Ching-wei. It is decided that Man-shu's body will be laid in the coffin at three o'clock this afternoon. At ten o'clock tomorrow morning, the bier will be moved [from the hospital] and placed temporarily at Kuang-ch'ao Cemetery [for Strangers]. (*MSCC*, V, 87)

This document represents a summary of Man-shu's accomplishments in life as well as the image he left among his friends and contemporaries. A member of the Southern Society, Wang Chao-ming (Wang Ching-wei) was at that time Sun Yat-sen's right-hand man, and later an important though controversial figure in the Nationalist government. Man-shu's intimate relationship with members of the revolutionary party is thus shown by the fact that Wang Chao-ming, who had only a casual acquaintance with the poet-monk, should have personally undertaken to make arrangements for the funeral.

It was not until June 9, 1924, that his Southern Society friends raised enough money to bury him belatedly but appropriately at a scenic spot at the foot of Orphan Hill along the southern shores of West Lake, a location he greatly loved in his lifetime. The cemetery plot was donated by a female member of the Southern Society, a close friend of Ch'en Ch'ü-ping, who also initiated a campaign for the erection of a monument and a mausoleum, the latter to be called the Swallow's Mausoleum, for the beloved poet-monk. An announcement of Man-shu's interment was carried in the same newspaper, as follows:

> A Notice on the Burial of the Reverend Man-shu at Orphan Hill: It has been ascertained that at nine on the morning of June 8, the train bearing the Reverend Man-shu's bier will depart from Shanghai at the North Station of the Shanghai-Nanking Railroad. It will reach Hangchow around four in the afternoon. All of Man-shu's friends in both cities who want to join the procession should wait at either of the two stations at the appointed time. The coffin will be interred at noon on June 9.
> Specially announced by members of the Southern Society. (*MSCC*, V, 90)

Although the lack of funds prevented the building of a mausoleum on the site, a stone monument, its inscription written in a beautiful classical style by a notable scholar of the Southern Society, was erected alongside the grave as a lasting memorial to this Sino-Japanese genius, an heir to unfulfilled accomplishments in the realms of poetry, fiction, and painting.

CHAPTER 8

An Heir of Unfulfilled Renown—An Epilogue

ALTHOUGH Su Man-shu died prematurely half a century ago, his works have survived the wreckage of the times and will long remain a part of the Chinese cultural heritage. We can now state with some assurance that he will be remembered as a major literary figure of the first two decades of the twentieth century. Posterity has come to revere him for his writings, which are substantial, considering his short span of life, and for a personality that endeared him to friends and readers alike.

As we have already seen, a number of his works were published during his lifetime, either in separate volumes or in newspapers and magazines. Man-shu was nevertheless careless about his own writings, as he was about his money and his health. Not long after his death, a serious effort was made to collect his works, which culminated in the publication in 1927 of *A Chronological Life of Su Man-shu and Other Articles* edited by Liu Wu-chi. In 1928, a five-volume *Complete Works of Man-shu* edited by Liu Ya-tzu and Liu Wu-chi was completed. Published in Shanghai by the Pei-hsin Book Company,[1] both works were well received by the public and their record sales attested to his continuing popularity among the general readership. Later reproduced in various forms by other publishers, the Pei-hsin volumes nevertheless have not yet been superseded,[2] and they remain the standard edition of his works. Some revisions and additions of new materials will be necessary to complete a definitive edition.

Of the new books that have appeared since then, the most important is *Man-shu's Literary Remains* (Pei-hsin, 1929), collected by Hsiao Jen-ch'iu and published by Liu Ya-tzu; the title inscription in four large characters was written by Sun Yat-sen. As has been mentioned earlier, this volume contains the miscellaneous notes and diaries; it also includes photographic reproductions of a number of pictures and articles of personal interest, such as name cards, a cassock, a Buddhist certificate, and a receipt for a coffin. Some entries and references in the diaries, however, are so obscure that they add further to the many unresolved riddles of Man-shu's private life.

The paintings, most of which he executed at the request of friends, were previously widely scattered. When the project to print his picture album by Ho Chen, Liu Shih-p'ei's wife, failed, Man-shu managed to have thirteen paintings reproduced for publication in the *People's Report* and the *Tien Yee News* in 1907, and nine in *Affinities in Literature* in 1908. But it was not until 1919, a year after his death, that Ts'ai Shou privately issued a small volume entitled *Wonderful Brushworks of the Reverend Man-shu* with a foreword by Chang Ping-lin. It contains reproductions of twenty-two paintings, five of which appeared previously in the *Tien Yee News* and seven in *Affinities in Literature.* A limited edition for circulation among friends and art connoisseurs, it soon became a rare collector's item. In the well-illustrated *Complete Works of Man-shu* and *Man-shu's Literary Remains* are to be found reproductions of over forty paintings by Man-shu. Altogether, deducting duplications, a total of seventy-odd extant pictures provides a good idea of the style and content of his art—mostly landscapes on scrolls and fans—but the poor quality and small size of the reproductions fail to do justice to the art of the painter. Already rare in the 1930's, the originals would now seem to be irretrievably lost, and even reprints are hard to obtain.

From both the literary and artistic works, insights into the character and thought of the poet-painter can be gained. Like his poetry, his pictures present an image of a creative artist richly endowed with imagination and sensitivity. But, while the poetry shows him to be a man of sentiment who, despite otherworldly yearnings, often yielded to the attractions of physical love and patriotic urgings, the paintings are even more ethereal and possess a magic touch of serene beauty that transforms the grubby commonness of life. On the other hand, the prose writings, both polemic essays and short stories, reveal the turbulent mind of a young idealist passionately concerned with social problems. Nonetheless, in all his creative works there is nothing incongruous in conception or feeling. These seeming contradictions merely point to the many-faceted nature of the man, in whom idealistic, romantic, and revolutionary sentiments came together. In moments of despair due to sickness and loneliness, his idealism sometimes degenerated into a profound pessimism or an obstinate disdain for human values. Although he critically favored Byron over Shelley, he seems to have been more like Shelley than Byron—an ineffectual angel, flapping his wings in vain.

Like Shelley he was ardently dedicated to revolutionary causes in early youth, yet he lacked lasting convictions and any understanding of the true nature of revolution, either in its nationalistic or ideological aspects. Typical of Chinese intellectuals in the pre-Republican period, he was hostile to the Manchu regime and was overjoyed at its overthrow, but he failed to adhere resolutely to his revolutionary faith once he became disillusioned with the course of political events after the revolution. Thus, youthful zeal quickly evaporated, giving way to political apathy and a growing disenchantment with life. The fiery young author who had once praised the patriotic deeds of brave officials and virtuous women in their resistance to the Manchu conquest, who had excoriated his fellow Cantonese for fawning servility toward westerners, who had deplored the Dutch oppression of Chinese communities in Java, who had re-echoed the woeful cries of the Indian people after the British conquest, who had sung passionately of Byron's "Isles of Greece," and who had glorified the American anarchist Emma Goldman, later became contrariwise an aimless wanderer who confined himself to making pretty but frivolous remarks on life and to discussing the affairs of "the flowers and the moon."[3] So well did Man-shu camouflage his true feelings that even Liu Ya-tzu was deceived when he once remarked: "Man-shu refused absolutely to talk about politics."

There were also perceptible changes in his attitude toward religion. Persistent in his hostility toward Christianity and Christian missionaries, only the Reverend Lopez (possibly the Reverend George Candlin?) was an exception. Even his fervor for Buddhism, like that for revolution, seems to have cooled considerably in the last years of his life. Apparently, he did not find it inconsistent to preach revolution and to espouse Buddhism at the same time. His dedication to the Buddhist faith reached its fullest development in 1908, when, after having issued with Chang Ping-lin "An Admonishment to All Buddhist Disciples" and "A Manifesto to Both Officials and Commoners," he went to Nanking to teach at the Jetavana School founded by Yang Wen-hui, the venerable Buddhist scholar. Soon afterward for reasons that have not yet been ascertained, his commitment to Buddhism seems to have subsided, and what might have made him the "Martin Luther of the Chinese Buddhist Reform Movement" never developed—this appelation was no more than an idealization by his panegyrists. To be sure, in speech and published writings he continued to keep alive the image of a Buddhist monk, but this appears to have been more a deliberate posture or façade than a true devotion to religion.

On matters pertaining to love and the opposite sex, his ideas are not only incongruous but also strangely paradoxical. The romantic lover in poetry and the sympathetic narrator of tragic love in fiction, he impresses one on the other hand as a follower of Schopenhauer in his denunciation of the female sex as "the source of calamity."[4] The translation of *An Account of My Refugee Life on the Seashores of Sala* contains a series of slanderous attacks on womanhood, where women are compared to poisonous serpents and hungry ghosts sent by hell to destroy man's spiritual body. Possibly an original work rather than a translation, these ideas may provisionally be credited to Su Man-shu. In certain instances, he was not only pessimistic but almost misanthropic, as when he wrote angrily to Liu Ya-tzu: "I say, one more Chinese student abroad will produce one more traitor to the country. . . . As for girls studying abroad, they would be better off if they learned how to act in an all-female vaudeville." Although utterances of this kind are rare in his collected writings, they are, nevertheless, what one may regard as manifestations of psychological abnormalities in a once fervent and open-minded young man who reacted violently in moments of bitter resentment against social evils.

These unusual strains in character notwithstanding, Man-shu won the esteem of his contemporaries for a pure and ingenuous manner. Seemingly an innocent child at heart, he roamed about nonchalantly, uncontaminated by the jealousies and contentions of men avaricious in their rivalries for power and position. This side of his nature was evident in all his relationships, and friends were fond of telling stories of his idiosyncrasies. Quite typical is the following account by Chang Ping-lin:

> Nevertheless, Man-shu had little understanding of human affairs. He even failed to distinguish the seasons for the planting of rice and wheat. He would often consume four to five bowls of rice without knowing that it came from the rice plants in the paddy fields. Frequently poor, he begged people for loans. Whenever he got a few silver dollars, he would spend

them on food; when he finished eating, the money too would be gone. Once, when he was in Japan, he ate five to six catties of crushed ice.[5] At night, he could hardly move. People thought that he was dead, but when they took a closer look he was still breathing. The next day, he continued to eat ice as before . . .

There was an obese American woman, weighing 400 catties, her shin as big as an earthen jar. When Man-shu met her, he asked, "If you were looking for a husband, how could you get a man to match you in size and weight?"

"What I would like to have," the woman replied, "is someone light and thin."

"How about me, then?" Man-shu said, "I am thin enough to be your mate."

He often acted like that.

But he was frank and straightforward by nature. When he met someone who was hypocritical or disgraceful in behavior, he would scold the man with angry looks. People thought that Man-shu was just crazy or idiotic; so they did not mind him.[6]

Apropos of this aspect of Man-shu's character, Liu Ya-tzu in the preface to the *Poetic Remains of the Swallow's Mausoleum* has perceptively observed: "People considered him half-witted, but whenever he was engaged in conversation, he always made his point with subtlety. Truly, Man-shu was no idiot!"[7]

Not long after his death, Man-shu became the target for all sorts of amusing tales, which grew taller with each telling. With so many stories about his gourmet habits, one simply has to regard epicurism as one of his besetting sins. It is said that he would remove the gold fillings from his teeth to exchange for candy, thus earning himself the nickname of the "sugar-coated monk," or, in a variant version, for Manila cigars, to which he was equally addicted. Often, these indulgences had dire consequences, as, for instance, when he was seized with a terrible stomachache after having stuffed himself on raw abalone in a Japanese restaurant. In other anecdotes, he is said to have gorged himself with sweet wheatcakes, or "eight-precious" glutinous rice, all Chinese delicacies which he loved.

He was also well known for his naïveté and absent-mindedness. In "Anecdotes of the Reverend Man-shu," Ma Chung-shu has written:

One day, Man-shu got several tens of one-dollar bills from a friend. In good spirits, he went to buy himself a blue cloth cassock at a store near

Little South Gate [in Shanghai]. Without asking the price, he paid the salesman twenty dollars. When the latter was about to tell him that he had overpaid, Man-shu, sailing down the street in his Buddhist robe, was already more than ten yards away from the store. The remaining bills he scattered here and there along the way. When he returned, his friend asked him what he had got with all this money. Man-shu could only show him a second-hand cassock and packages of cigars.[8]

The following episode was told by Hu Yün-yü, the elder brother of Hu Huai-ch'en and also a member of the Southern Society:

One day, as I was going to a friend's house for a dinner party, I met Man-shu on the way.

"Where are you going?" I asked.

"To a friend's party," he answered.

"Where?"

"I don't know."

"Who invited you?"

"I don't know."

Man-shu turned around to ask me, "Where are you going?"

"To a friend's party."

"Let's go together, then," he said. When we got there, Man-shu started to eat without first presenting himself to the host.

Actually, it was not my friend but somebody else who invited Man-shu.[9]

Despite these oddities in character, Man-shu was befriended and beloved by all who came to know him. They had compassion for his misery and suffering, respected his moral integrity, and admired his literary and artistic talents. Almost unanimously they had fond memories of this poet-monk who lived the life of a "lone swan." None spoke harshly of him, and all praised his ability to remain aloof from the ugliness around him, his "pure white plumage" unsullied and unclipped, as it were. Even such an uncompromising critic and severe taskmaster as Chang Ping-lin, who could speak slightingly of Sun Yat-sen and Huang Hsing, had only kind words for his young friend:

Of the scholars of Kwangtung, Chien Chao-liang among the Confucianists and Su Man-shu among the Buddhists may be said to have possessed lofty virtues that reached high to the clouds. Next come fellows such as Huang Chieh. As for those people who brag of their high positions on account of party connections, they are not to be mentioned in the same breath with Man-shu.

Formerly, Man-shu was on friendly terms with Liu Shih-p'ei and often stayed at Liu's house. But he railed at those who secretly plotted with Liu, and refused to sit together with them. "Pounded, he does not break apart: thrown into the slime, he is unsullied by filth"; this may be said of Man-shu. He did not join any political faction[10] because he disdained it. Therefore many who were political-minded resented him. When the news of Liu Shih-p'ei's spying for the Manchu government broke, they used the occasion to slander Man-shu. These critics, however, failed to compare their own worth with his. With a small measure of virtue and one hundredth of his talent, they were not good enough to hold the riding whip for him. When Man-shu can be disparaged, then the universe perhaps will have reached its end![11]

While Man-shu's moral character, as we have seen, earned the respect of his contemporaries, they were equally amazed at the rapid development of his talent for writing and painting in the course of a few years. He won much admiration for his artistic ability. Numerous anecdotes have been told and often repeated of how his friends and admirers besieged him with requests for paintings. At other times, he sketched when he was seized with inspiration. Recollecting Man-shu's visit to their country home in suburban Shanghai in the fifth month of 1912, Lu Ling-su, the wife of Liu San, provides the following account: "One evening after dinner, Man-shu asked for some rouge for painting. At that time, as all the children had gone to bed, my husband did not want to disturb them. So he got Man-shu only a thin cake of rouge and placed it in a tray. While talking and laughing, Man-shu finished in an instant a picture of the Pavilion of the Yellow Leaves and a landscape for my folding fan. Then he dipped his pen into black ink to paint a horizontal scroll. As the rouge had not been removed from the tip of the pen, the withered willows and lonely crows, all maroon colored, presented a wonderful view. We have kept the pictures all these years."[12] This eyewitness description of the artist at work reveals the casual but ingenious manner in which Man-shu painted his pictures. From the last painting, for instance, we gain a clear idea of how he succeeded in reproducing with a few strokes of the brush the simple beauties of nature, represented here by rippling waters, distant mountains, and wilted willows.

Among the finer lanscapes by Man-shu are "Autumn Willows at the White Gate (Nanking)," drawn for Liu San; "Mourning One's Dreams on the Banks of Lake Fen," for Yeh Ch'u-ts'ang; and "An Old Fisherman Among Rivers and Lakes," for Ch'eng

Yen-sheng, his friend at Anhwei High School in An-ch'ing. In these and other pictures are represented his favorite scenes of mountain peaks, precipitous rocks, lonely pines, weeping willows, and a waning moon. These and solitary landscapes portraying desolate city walls, a distant pagoda or monastery, thatched cottages, or a broken bridge are sometimes animated by an old fisherman, an aged monk, a plowing ox, or a spirited steed. In his youth, he also drew pictures of historical figures, such as heroes and beautiful women. One such painting features Lin Tai-yü burying flowers, a scene from the novel *Dream of the Red Chamber*. Viewed as a whole, his art shows little trace of Western or Japanese influence, although he was doubtlessly familiar with these traditions. On the other hand, while following in the footsteps of the landscape masters of the Sung and Yüan dynasties, he brought to Chinese painting an originality and conception all his own. His art is so unique and transcendental that it can be better seen and appreciated than described in words. Encomia by his friends, who were not trained art critics, are useful as personal impressions rather than as critical evaluations. Ho Chen perhaps came closer to discovering the secret of his art than anyone else when she wrote in her postscript to an unpublished album of his paintings: "My teacher, having penetrated the depths of the doctrine of the 'mere heart,' engaged himself, whenever he was unoccupied with intellectual pursuits, in the art of painting. The pictures he drew were mostly scenes of natural phenomena created through the heart and are particularly remarkable for their spiritual rhythm. From this we infer that all objects in the three worlds are products of the consciousness. The scenes in his pictures were phenomena conjured up in the artist's consciousness and then reproduced in visual form on white silk."[13] It is for this reason that Man-shu's pictures, transcending both the realities of nature and life, attain an ethereal beauty rarely found in modern Chinese painting.

Intellectually, Man-shu was only a country bumpkin when he first entered Ta-t'ung School in Yokohama, and his senior schoolmates like Feng Tzu-yu had little regard for his scholarly abilities. Nor did he distinguish himself later as a student at Waseda University in Tokyo, notwithstanding a certain industry and perseverance. When he returned to Shanghai at the age of twenty as a newspaper hack, his Chinese prose style was so poor that his colleagues had to polish it for him. It was not until 1907 when, inspired by Chang Ping-lin and others, he first made a serious attempt to write poetry. Already twenty-four at the time, he was still a novice in a country where precociousness in versification was relatively common. But, in the short span of seven years from 1907 to 1914, he managed to produce some of the best Chinese poetry of the period. To be sure, when compared with the vast quantities of poetry composed by his friends of the Southern Society during a comparable period, his poetic output was small, totaling only some ninety verses. Nonetheless, while most of these poets have been forgotten by posterity, Su Man-shu alone continues to enjoy both popularity and critical acclaim.

Critics generally attribute his success as a poet to genius, that illusive and unfathomable natural capacity for creative expression possessed more by some than others. That he was endowed with a certain genius is true, but one still has to delve deeper into his poetry to discover those qualities which distinguish his verse. First of all, it must be observed that he was by no means a great poet in the sense that Li Po, Tu Fu, and Su Shih were. His work is limited mainly to one form of Chinese poetry, the *ch'i-chüeh* or seven-word four-line stanza. In this particular poetic form, however, his achievement was outstanding. Comprising a total of only twenty-eight words, the *ch'i-chüeh* is in one sense the easiest form to employ, but also the most difficult to use well. Very few poets excelled in this form, which attained its highest development at the hands of the T'ang dynasty masters. Even the Sung poets, who branched out into other domains of Chinese poetry, failed to match the T'ang poets in this respect. Therefore, one risks the criticism of partiality in asserting that some of Man-shu's best *ch'i-chüeh* rank with the best T'ang poems in the same form, but this is nonetheless a critical assessment arrived at after due consideration and held with conviction.

Not all Man-shu's poems are of the highest quality. Quite a few are professedly imitations of late T'ang poetry and are often marred by clichés, conceits, artificiality, and excessive elaboration in description and overuse of image and metaphor. At times, he was not averse to borrowing from the earlier poets. This practice has of course long been commonly accepted; for anyone who falls under the magic spell of great poetry—there is such a considerable amount of it in the Chinese tradition—will consciously or unconsciously retain or adopt fine expressions and beautiful images as a part of his own poetic vocabulary. Finally, to a strict prosodist, Man-shu's versification may seem faulty in a number of instances, but then the T'ang poets themselves took liberties with the rules of prosody whenever it suited their individual purposes.

What one can do, therefore, is to discover and identify the lyrical elements in his verse. Briefly, these can be listed as naturalness, a sensitivity to beauty, and a spontaneous flow of emotion. Naturalness as an element of his style is sometimes deceptive, as his poems also reveal a subtlety that is scarcely noticeable in a superficial reading. The Chinese fondness for erudite words and obscure references can sometimes be construed as a façade to hide a paucity of emotions and ideas. Man-shu's limited scholarship and his disinclination to employ literary devices should not however be considered as a weakness. In contrast to the works of the expert versifiers of the Southern Society, his poems are remarkably devoid of literary allusions, and the few that intrude into his lines appear delightfully amateurish in tone. One gains, on the other hand, a clear impression of natural ease in the expression of personal feelings, though this does not preclude an ingenious use of poetic devices. Compare, for instance, the following two poems:

(1)

Ask me not whether our parting is for life or death!
A lonely monk, I wander like clouds floating and waters flowing.
For no reason at all, I madly laugh and then loudly wail.
Although a warm and glad heart I had, it is as cold as ice.
—To Ch'en Tu-hsiu as I Pass by Wakamatsu-cho in a State of Emotion

(2)

Spring rain pattering on an upper chamber—the sound of a "foot-and-eight flute."
How I yearn to go to watch the tide at Ch'ien-t'ang!
With straw sandals and a broken alms-bowl, all unknown I roamed.
I wonder how many bridges I've crossed, where the cherry blossoms bloom.
—Occasional Poem, No. 1

Alike in their expression of a prevailing mood of sadness, the poems differ greatly in the way the emotional state is revealed. The first poem is a plain statement of the poet's melancholy that arises from a lonely and wandering life, whereas in the second the same mood is conjured up in a subtle, artistic manner through the use of associations and intimations. "Spring Rain on an Upper Chamber" is the title of a popular melody for the long flute which, introduced from China, can still be heard in Japan. Its melancholy sound arouses in the poet, as he passes by the house of an unseen flute player in a drizzling rain, a sense of loneliness and desolation. In turn it gives rise to a nostalgic feeling for his home country, especially at a time when the tide at Ch'ien-t'ang near the scenic city of Hangchow presents a spectacular view and an occasion for joy when watching it in the company of friends. But here on foreign soil, his plight as a mendicant monk, unknown as the flute player is unseen, contrasts vividly with the cheerful view of the cherry blossoms.

While his poetry reveals a sensitivity to the beauties of nature, it is also enlivened with a human touch. Just as the scenery he describes is always delightfully charming and exquisite, rather than grand and majestic, so the feelings he expresses are tranquil and serene, in keeping with the landscape and often blending with it. The following poems, both quoted before, are worth citing again as examples of his achievement in this respect:

Amidst the dense white clouds which embrace Thunder Peak,
Stand a few wintry plum trees, their red blooms clothed with snow.
After a vegetable repast I sink slowly, completely into a deep meditation,
As the sound of a distant bell falls on shadows in the monastery pool.
—Written during My Stay at White Clouds Monastery at West Lake

Deep under the willow's canopying shadows the horse treads proudly,
Where a vast expanse of silvery sand pursues the ebbing tide.
The ice-flag atop a thatched store signals the nearby market;
The red leaves on the mountain top the lasses gather for firewood.
—Passing by Kamata

In both poems, the scenery is unspoiled but enlivened by human presence as man and nature learn to live in harmony with each other. The same kind of happy interaction and affinity between the two is shown in the following highly imaginative lines:

Riding a lean horse, I need not worry about the long road ahead—
The peach blossoms, so lovely red, yearn to come up to my singing whip.
—Singing on My Way to Yodoe

In all these instances, the charms of nature gently strike a responsive chord in the heart of the poet.

Likewise, one finds a soft rippling of the emotions in a number of his poems. To be sure, he did sometimes abandon himself to violent passions, as when he chanted and wailed over Byron's poems when boating in the moonlight; nevertheless, in his own verse, he speaks in a calm and restrained voice even while giving vent to strong personal emotion:

At this moment, even if I am full of emotion and tears,
I'll talk randomly on topics that range from the sea of men to men in heaven.
—Poems without Titles, No. 6

I can only give back to you, dear maiden, an alms-bowl of unfeeling tears,
Regretting that I did not meet you before my head was shaved.
—Occasional Poems, No. 4

Please do not ask me, when we meet, about affairs in this mortal world.
The old country so grieves my heart that only tears flow.
—Nineteen Miscellaneous Poems Written during My Sojourn in Japan, No. 2

In these three selections, be it fond memories of a childhood sweetheart, internal conflict between love and religion, or sorrow for the grievous situation in his own country, the outpouring of emotion is kept under control, so that there is tranquility and placidness on the surface, notwithstanding currents of agitated feelings underneath. It is only by reading between the lines that one comes to realize what a passionately sentimental individual he must have been.

A large number of Man-shu's poems are about friendship, love, and feminine charms, themes that have been explored repeatedly by Chinese poets throughout the ages. Man-shu seems to have been especially captivated by seductive feminine traits. There is nothing lascivious in his poetry, yet he took nonetheless a keen interest in the toilet, hairdo, gestures, and movements of beautiful women. An expert on feminine coiffure—he once collected and sketched a hundred styles of the ancient period[14]—he was particularly keen on the description of hair styles:

Dabbing lightly her moth eyebrows, she comes to pay her respects to the master painter,
Her elegant hairknot, shaped like a twin-heart, bound together by black silk.
—*On Painting the Portrait of a Harpsichord Player, Poem 2*

A lotus hairdo aslant her head,[15] *with lovely looks and lustrous hair,*
She imprinted her powdered fingers on a green bamboo book.
—Title Lost

Examples of other lines on the attractions of lovely women are "Her slendor, willowy waist, most lovely to behold"; "Her cheeks blooming and her lips enticing,[16] she sits, playing the mouth organ"; "On her arms linger faintly a trace of beancurd fragrance"; "As she fondles her silken girdle, putting to shame the pale maiden in the moon." The following poem is a good example of his portrayal of a blooming, vivacious, but bashful girl:

Having changed into a silken shirt, she descends from the western chamber,
Like the warm fragrance of a tender bloom,[17] *and keeps on talking.*
But when one inquires about her age, she becomes even more bashful.
Behind the crystal screen she goes to practice on the lute.
—*Nineteen Miscellaneous Poems Written during My Sojourn in Japan, No. 3*

In addition to their lyrical qualities, these poems have a charm of their own derived from the poet's experiences in Japan and his Buddhist background, which, in turn, lends these verses an exotic coloration. The figures of the ice-flag on the thatched store, the cherry-blossom bridges, the foot-and-eight flute have been mentioned previously as typical of the Japanese scene. Also numerous are references to Buddhism, in which Man-shu found consolation, a contemplative peace of mind, and a source of exhilaration in this fleeting life. Religion triumphed over love in his life and poetry, and a total surrender to the Buddhist faith is indicated in the following stanza:

A mind in meditation cares not for the envy of the moth-eyebrowed.
In Buddha's precept a common origin have anger and affection.
Wearing a rain-hat and a cloak of mist, I shall return whence I came,
Without a trace of love or hate for my fellow man.

Religion also inspires the following "Note to Fan-jen," a fellow monk:

> *Let's get drunk with the dew on a golden stem,*
> *And paint with rouge the peony blossoms.*
> *Here, fallen petals pile up a foot deep;*
> *There is no need to bring along a prayer mat.*

The clever blending of natural setting with art and religion in the poem produces a delightful effect, making this poem something of a perfect little gem. Thus, one gets tipsy on his poetry, on the "dew on a golden stem"; it exhilarates but does not intoxicate.

In my opinion, his contributions lie more in the realm of poetry than prose, although the latter looms much larger in bulk. His prose writings can be divided into three categories: (1) miscellaneous notes and essays, (2) letters, and (3) stories. Except for the general knowledge they impart and the information they provide about his personal feelings and thoughts, the random notes and prefaces are not particularly noteworthy as works of literature, while the early political essays are immature in content and crude in language. On the other hand, his letters are among the best of his writings and rank high in epistolary style in a literature long noted for this genre. Specimens of his letters, mostly of a biographical nature, have been given in previous sections. It suffices to state here that these letters bear the distinct stamp of his genius with their exquisite style and fine phraseology, humor and warmth of feeling, delicate touches of sentimentality, and intimate revelations of personality. In the preface to the *Poetic Remains of the Swallow's Mausoleum,* Liu Ya-tzu tells us: "Man-shu was fond of writing in a fine calligraphy on pink stationery, his characters as small as the head of a fly. His letters have grace and elegance, but they are often colored by melancholy and sentimentality. Like the poet of yore, he had a bellyful of grievances against the times" (*MSCC*, IV, 83).

The Lone Swan and other stories have already been discussed in some detail. As a whole, they excel with respect to literary style, the expression of personal sentiment, and the presentation of conflict, either internal or external. However, the weaknesses of these stories are also obvious and many. Some of them are cluttered with long series of episodes that weaken the plot and dilute the characterization, both of which cannot be said to have been his strong points. Digressions and lengthy discourses hamper the movement of the plot and create a sense of artificiality. *The Lone Swan*, for instance, could gain in intensity and unity if pruned of extraneous matters. The same view is expressed by Yü Ta-fu in his "Miscellaneous Criticism of Man-shu's Writings" (1927). While several inaccuracies in Yü's summary of the plot indicate the casual manner of his criticism, as a whole the general arguments advanced are well taken and valid. Apparently unaware of the fact that the novel was left unfinished and that the last sentence is a later addition, Yü Ta-fu takes Man-shu to task for the poor ending of the novel. He also criticizes "Tale of a Broken Hairpin" for its inferior narrative technique and inadequate character delineation: "Man-shu uses a semi-realistic form of narration, which constantly reminds the reader of the fictitious nature of his plot. In this story, especially weak is the connection between the hero's character and the plot development; something is amiss in the sequence of cause and effect. Sometimes, to arouse the reader's expectations and curiosity, he employs a form of suspense which, however, is not in keeping with techniques adopted by talented modern writers familiar with Western fiction; rather, it is a method used by the popularizers of vulgar and tawdry stories."[18] Similarly, Henry McAleavy comments that "Tale of a Broken Hairpin" makes strange reading today.[19]

If we view Man-shu's stories from a historical perspective, we shall be able to appreciate them better and to understand that their limitations and failings are typical of the fiction of the times. It is true that Man-shu, who must have dipped widely into Western novels, failed to take advantage of more sophisticated methods of narration and character delineation developed by English and European writers of the nineteenth century; but he was essentially a poet, a romancer, who was interested primarily in presenting the emotions of love in a language both expressive and eloquent. Granted that there are certain absurdities in situation and morbidity of sentiment in his fiction, these are but minor flaws when compared to the "cheap, tawdry materials" commonly found in the so-called Mandarin Duck and Butterfly School of Fiction that was in vogue at that time. It is also true that he failed to learn from the best traditions of native storytelling, which are to be found in the *Dream of the Red Chamber*, with which we have compared *The Lone Swan* for certain similarities of theme. These faults may mar his stories, but they fall far short of the moral depravity mentioned by Hu Shih in his letter to Ch'ien Hsüan-t'ung of November 20, 1917: "You have frequently praised Su Man-shu's stories. For this reason, when I was in Shanghai last time, I got a copy of his stories and read them carefully, but failed to discover anything worthwhile in them. 'A Tale of Crimson Silk' is filled with bestial sensuality. It also drags in rather unnecessarily quite a bit of irrelevant material to pad the story. This is due to our present evil practice of paying so much money per thousand words. 'A Tale on the Burning of the Sword' is a work of sheer nonsense. It is worth less than one hundredth of the *Strange Stories from a Chinese Studio*. So what merits could it have?"[20]

Aside from the matter of personal opinion, which we will not dispute, Hu Shih is unfair in his criticism in two respects: First, it is strange that a careful reading of "A Tale of Crimson Silk" should have produced in the critic a sense of "bestial sensuality." Su Man-shu's tales may be criticized for a number of reasons, but certainly not for a description of animal passion, and least of all "A Tale of Crimson Silk." Secondly, Man-shu wrote both stories mentioned by Hu Shih specifically for his friend, Chang Shih-chao, and to accuse the author of pecuniary considerations in this instance represents a complete failure to understand Man-shu's character and his motivations in this case, the latter being clearly set forth by Chang Shih-chao and Ch'en Tu-hsiu in their prefaces to these stories.

Yü Ta-fu stated that much of the fad for Man-shu in the mid-1920's came about as a reaction among young writers against the omission of Su Man-shu's name from Hu Shih's "Chinese Literature of the Last Fifty Years" (1872–1922), in which Hu Shih ignored altogether the poets of the Southern Society. On the other hand, according to Yü Ta-fu, groups of ardent youths, "after having read Man-shu's beautifully sad verses and being struck by his eccentric behavior, were seized with a frantic zeal to worship him blindly. They considered everything Man-shu wrote to be superior and his position to be even higher than that of Li Po and Ch'ü Yüan."[21] Between the two extremes represented by Hu Shih on the one hand and the youths of the time on the other, critics like Yü Ta-fu and Chou Tso-jen steered a middle course. As morbidly sentimental in his own stories as Man-shu was in his poetry, Yü Ta-fu ranked Man-shu's poetry, especially his translations, much higher than his fiction. A highly respected literary figure until his collaboration with the Peking puppet regime during the Japanese occupation, Chou Tso-jen, together with his elder brother Chou Shu-jen (Lu Hsün), was the editor of the *Yü-ssu* weekly (1924–30), one of the leading literary periodicals of the time. In 1926 and 1927, it published articles on Su Man-shu by Liu Ya-tzu and Liu Wu-chi and their correspondence with Man-shu's friends and admirers. The space given these articles and miscellanea was extensive enough to provoke the protest of one reader. In reply, Chou Tso-jen maintained that Man-shu's ideas were commonplace enough, but his poems and essays, objectively speaking, were well written, and much better than the writings of scholars who professed their loyalty to the previous regime (the Manchu dynasty). "Man-shu's writings," wrote Chou Tso-jen, "contain a genuine spirit and sincere manner that reveal clearly his personality. Therein lie his merits."[22] Regarding Man-shu as a writer of the "Mandarin Duck and Butterfly School of Fiction," a school given to decadent ideas widely popular in the first two decades of the twentieth century, Chou Tso-jen believed that Man-shu was a great master of that school, but weighed down by the tawdry and lurid writings of its lesser writers, "just as Confucius was by his disciples," and that in this fashion his natural abilities were somewhat obscured.[23]

In the decade from 1927 to 1937, Man-shu's influence was widespread, and in certain instances this influence was far from salutary. As has been indicated earlier, efforts by Liu Ya-tzu and Liu Wu-chi to study Man-shu and to reconstruct the details of his life aroused a favorable response from the public. Tangible evidence of this new interest in the life and writings of Man-shu is to be found in the numerous reminiscences, essays, and poems written about him during this period. These constitute the bulk of the *Chronological Life of Su Man-shu and Other Articles* (1927), as well as the two volumes of *Appendices* in the five-volume edition of the *Complete Works of Man-shu* (Pei-hsin, 1928). Subsequently, Liu Ya-tzu collected another one hundred such items on Man-shu, thirty-two of which he considered important enough for publication,[24] but the printing was delayed by the Sino-Japanese War and the manuscript is now to be presumed lost. Among the unhappy effects of Man-shu's writings on the younger generation, a tragic example was the suicide of his niece Su Shao-ch'iung, a sixteen-year-old schoolgirl, on March 10, 1928, in Kobe, Japan.[25]

The vogue for Man-shu came to a sudden halt with the Sino-

Japanese War (1937–45), and it failed to revive after the occupation of mainland China by the Chinese Communist party in 1949. Nonetheless, there have been occasional additions during this period to the critical literature. Public demand for his works prompted a Chungking bookseller to approach Liu Wu-chi, who edited a *Memorial Volume of the Reverend Man-shu's Works* in 1943. In 1949, *A Critical Biography of Su Man-shu* was published in Shanghai by Huang Ming-ch'i. More recently, his works have been reprinted in Hong Kong, mostly from Wen Kung-chih's edition of the *Complete Works of the Reverend Man-shu.*[26] In 1965, *Man-shu's Poems and Imitations of Man-shu's Poems*, compiled by Chiang I-an, the author of most of these "imitation-poems,"[27] appeared in Taipei, Taiwan. Hong Kong newspapers and periodicals frequently publish notes on the life and times of Man-shu and his friends. The most important of these to date is the article "Su Man-shu's Poetry Album," which contains two hitherto unpublished poems by Man-shu;[28] it also includes a number of poems inscribed on the "Album" by Pao T'ien-hsiao and Chang Shih-chao, the oldest of Man-shu's four surviving friends.[29] Although most of the poems purported to be by Man-shu discovered since the publication of the 1928 *Complete Works* have turned out to be forgeries, these two poems are authentic and valuable additions to the poet's meager poetic remains.[30]

Abroad, Su Man-shu is well known in Japan, where a number of Japanese writers, notably Satô Haruo, Ikeda Takashi, Masuda Wataru, and Yonezawa Hideo, have at one time or another studied and translated his works. In addition to *The Lone Swan*, "A Tale of Crimson Silk" and "The Tale on the Burning of the Sword" have been translated into Japanese by Iizuka Akira. In October, 1934, Satô Haruo (1892–1964), once a prominent literary figure, contributed an article to the *Literary Chronicle (Bungei Shunju)* entitled "What Kind of Person Was Su Man-shu?" in which he utilized new biographical data discovered by Liu Ya-tzu. The occasion for the article was a round-table conference to commemorate the contributions of Japanese writers of the modern period, such as Tokutomi Kenjiro, Natsume Soseki, and Moku A Mi. The contributions of Su Man-shu to modern letters were discussed in that context. Sponsored by the *Literary Chronicle* group, the conference was held at the Mitsukoshi department store in the Nihonbashi district in Tokyo, September 20–27, 1934. In conjunction with the meeting, there was also an exhibition of the various authors' manuscripts, books, and personal mementos; in Man-shu's case, his poems, paintings, and calligraphy, as well as his cassock, were on display. Following an earlier interpretation of Liu Ya-tzu, the Japanese had regarded Man-shu as a fellow countryman, and it was to refute this idea that Satô Haruo wrote his article with materials supplied by Masuda Wataru (b. 1903), and still later by Ikeda Takashi. The former, an admirer of Man-shu, went to Shanghai in 1931 to interview Lu Hsün (whose *Short History of Chinese Fiction* he had translated into Japanese). At that time, Lu Hsün presented Masuda with a copy of Liu Ya-tzu's *Complete Works of Man-shu* (1928). It should be added here that, according to Masuda, Man-shu was one of several "poor scholars" who, in 1907, joined Lu Hsün in an attempt to found in Tokyo a literary periodical to be called *Vita Nuova (Hsin-sheng)*—a project doomed to failure for a lack of financial support. The article "Su Man-shu's Life and Works" (1933?) by Yonezawa Hideo (b. 1905) was later translated into Chinese, as was Iizuka Akira's "Essay on Man-shu" (1936). Now a professor of Chinese at Hokkaido University, Iizuka Akira (b. 1907) earned his college degree in 1934 with a two-hundred-page thesis on Su Man-shu. Iizuka has since become the foremost Japanese authority on Man-shu, to whose study he contributed copiously from 1936 to 1965.[31]

Henry McAleavy, the British sinologist, was the first to introduce Su Man-shu to the Western reader. His book, *Su Man-shu, A Sino-Japanese Genius* (1960), grew out of a lecture originally delivered before the China Society in London on June 26, 1957. This attracted the attention of Liu Wu-chi, who subsequently read a paper, "The True Su Man-shu," at the 1961 meeting of the Association for Asian Studies, mainly to defend himself against McAleavy's criticism of his part in creating "legends" about the life and works of Su Man-shu, chiefly questions pertaining to Su's Japanese parentage, the Reverend Lopez, and the *Sanskrit Grammar*. Five years later, in another paper entitled "Three Chinese Versions of Byron's 'Isles of Greece' " and read at another meeting of the same association, Liu compared Man-shu's translation of the English poem with those of Ma Chün-wu and Hu Shih and concluded as follows: "In matters of poetic quality, Su Man-shu's translation seems to excel in the regularity of its meter and form, in the compactness and artistry of its language, and in an abundance of beautiful and quotable lines. Even though several of Su Man-shu's expressions are obscure and a part of his diction is archaic, as has been pointed out by Hu Shih, one should have little difficulty in understanding and appreciating his version of Byron's poem." Ramon Woon and Irving Y. C. Lo have labeled Man-shu the last of the great Ch'ing dynasty poets.[32] Their assessment of his contribution to Chinese letters is as follows: "As Yen Fu was the chief importer of Western social science in the late nineteenth century and Lin Shu, the great translator of Western fiction, Su Man-shu must be accorded the third place in this trinity of translators for his introduction of Western poetry, particularly for his work on Byron and Shelley who profoundly influenced him."[33]

While we have already surveyed Man-shu's contributions to creative writing, it seems proper in this connection to define his role as a translator. As we know, he was the first Chinese writer to translate Byron and Shelley, whose names were only vaguely known in China in the first decade of the present century. Man-shu wrote enthusiastically of them and called both poets of love and liberty, ideals which also inspired him in his own writings. A decade later, members of the Creation Society like Kuo Mo-jo and others came once again under the influence of Byron and Shelley, but even at the height of the New Literature Movement, no Chinese translator appeared to rival Man-shu's dedication to Byron. His *Selected Poems of Byron* is still the only important volume of Chinese translations from the English poet. Man-shu was also attracted to the great novels of the West, particularly Victor Hugo's *Les Misérables* and Dumas fils's *La Dame aux camélias*. Though he failed to translate the latter and did poorly with respect to the former, he nevertheless extended the horizon of Chinese knowledge of Western literature by his writings, just as he brought to the general reader's attention Western efforts in translating Chinese poetry. His chief contribution in this vein was as a promoter of cultural exchange between East and West. With four published works (*Affinities in Literature*, 1908; *Selected Poems of Byron*, 1909; *Voices of the Tide*, 1911; *Esoteric Essences of Chinese-English Poetry*, 1914) to his credit, he was both a pioneer translator of English poetry and an outstanding anthologist of Chinese poetry in English translation. As such, he contributed to the furtherance of East-West literary relationships long before his countrymen were aware of foreign literature and its merits and significance.

Indeed posterity has chosen not to forget Su Man-shu as his fame continues to spread: perhaps the most important testimony to his greatness as a national and literary figure is found in more recent publications in Taiwan and mainland China, the sites of two politically hostile Chinese regimes. In Taiwan, government publications honored Su Man-shu by including his works among those of the revolutionary writers of the Nationalist party when it celebrated in 1966 the centennial of Sun Yat-sen's birth. Likewise, in a large volume, *Biographies of the Revolutionary Martyrs and Early Revolutionists* (Taipei, 1965, pp. 881–82), his biography appears with those of his numerous friends who are now hailed as martyrs and heroes of the Nationalist Revolution.[34] While the friendly reception accorded Su Man-shu in Nationalist China is to be expected, it comes as a surprise that he should have received recognition in two recent histories of Chinese literature, compiled separately by groups of students in two universities (the National Peking University in Peking and the Fu-tan University in Shanghai) and published respectively in 1958 and 1959 in Communist China. He is mentioned in both works as a writer of the Southern Society, which is accorded treatment in a subsection in the last chapter of each history.[35] Regarding the Southern Society as the literary vanguard of the Chinese revolutionary movement, both histories focus their discussion on the poets, while making a distinction between the Southern Society novelists such as Su Man-shu and those of the "Mandarin Duck and Butterfly School." As a poet, he is criticized for his pessimism and Buddhist resignation, but he is also praised for his revolutionary spirit and zeal: "Su Man-shu is therefore a rather complicated poet, a romanticist in whom are intricately entangled negative and positive elements. An affirmative value should be assigned to his poems that express definitely revolutionary thoughts and patriotic spirit. But in Man-shu himself the weaknesses of the capitalistic class were also embodied, which are reflected in his poems of Buddhist escapism and sentimental vagaries. In a revolutionary era, these poems show a certain degree of backwardness. His poetry, therefore, cannot be regarded as the main product of the Southern Society."[36]

Despite these reservations, Su Man-shu assuredly occupies a nook in China's literary history, even when these histories are compiled from a strictly socialistic point of view. Thus the epilogue to his life may be concluded by saying that in the last fifty years Su Man-shu has influenced two generations of the Chinese people, by whom he will be remembered not as "a figure of legend" but as an early revolutionary and a talented writer of unfulfilled renown. The product of a transitional age that was listless in mood, turbulent in thought, throbbing with adventures, and yet filled with great expectations, he was a literary figure whose writings created more than a ripple in the mainstream of early twentieth-century Chinese literature. He personifies a happy union of the age-old literary traditions of China with the fresh invigorating romanticism of the West. His greatest asset, however, is his genial and genuine personality, which gives to all that he wrote, sang, and painted a touch of the beautiful, compounded of sensitivity, spontaneity, and childlike simplicity. A poet-monk, he subscribed to a faith that does not deny to its followers the enjoyment of secular life but recognizes also its concomitant sorrows and miseries.

Notes and References

Chapter One

1. Ch'en Kuo-ch'üan, whose Japanese mother was a close friend of Kawai, studied with Man-shu at Ta-t'ung School in Yokohama and was present at meetings between Man-shu and Kawai in 1907. When he was interviewed in Hong Kong in February, 1966, by Lo Hsiao-ming, another former Ta-t'ung student now in business in Yokohama, Ch'en revealed this story. I am indebted to Lo for this and other information on Man-shu's early life in Japan.

2. According to another account, Su Chieh-sheng left Japan in 1894 on account of the Sino-Japanese War. See Henry McAleavy, *Su Man-shu, A Sino-Japanese Genius* (London, 1960), p. 2.

3. See Feng Tzu-yu, "Ta-t'ung School at Yokohama," *Ko-ming i-shih* (Taipei, 1965), I, 76.

Chapter Two

1. Feng Tzu-yu, "Chang T'ai-yen and the Commemoration Meeting of China's Conquest (by the Manchus)," *op. cit.*, I, 86.

2. Feng Tzu-yu, "The Association for the People's Military Education in Tokyo," *op. cit.*, I, 163.

3. T'ang Kuo-tun is probably the same man as T'ang Chüeh-tun, a teacher at Ta-t'ung School.

4. i.e., *Man-shu ch'üan-chi (Complete Works of Man-shu)* edited by Liu Ya-tzu and Liu Wu-chi (Shanghai, 1928). Henceforth, all references to Man-shu's writings (except his poems, for which no citations will be given) will be to this standard edition (*MSCC*), which will be indicated parenthetically in the text. For the sake of convenience and whenever feasible, biographical data by his friends will also be footnoted in the same way.

5. In "The Real Su Man-shu," Feng Tzu-yu provides the following account: "While still a young man, his father Chieh-sheng had already betrothed him to a girl in the village. Now, when Chieh-sheng heard of his son's return to Hong Kong, he went there to fetch him, with the purpose of consummating the marriage ceremony. Man-shu however avoided his father. Believing Man-shu to be cold and ungrateful by nature, Ch'en Shao-pai remonstrated with him and strongly urged him to return home

with his father. Man-shu then left Ch'en without saying goodby. No one was informed of his whereabouts. Several months later, when he returned to Hong Kong, he had already shaved his head to become a monk and changed his name to Man-shu." Feng, *op. cit.*, I, 241.

Chapter Three

1. The same picture was found in the possession of one of Man-shu's friends, who lent it to Liu Ya-tzu for publication in his *Complete Works of Su Man-shu, A Popular Edition* (Shanghai: K'ai-hua Book Company, 1933).

2. I have translated *chu-chia* literally as "to leave home," although its proper meaning, as intended here, is "to become a monk."

3. Ch'en Kuo-ch'üan attended these meetings at Man-shu's request to help him in the conversation, since Man-shu's spoken Japanese was apparently rusty at the time. Ch'en Kuo-ch'üan gave this valuable information to Lo Hsiao-ming in October, 1966. I have omitted many details in my account and made one change—the time of the meeting—to fit into the known facts from other sources.

4. This could have been the source of the unutterable pangs of Man-shu's life, to which he constantly referred. The warm relationship between mother and son continued until Man-shu's death in 1918. Kawai died in 1923 in the catastrophic earthquake that devastated a large part of Tokyo and Yokohama.

5. This agrees with Man-shu's own statement (in his preface to the album) that he went three times (1898–1903, 1906, 1907) to Japan and once (1907) paid his respects to his mother.

6. In 1905 and 1906, the Association for the Preservation of National Learning published the following textbooks by Liu Shih-p'ei: *Chinese History* (2 vols.), *Chinese Classics* (2 vols.), *Chinese Literature* (1 vol.), *Chinese Geography* (2 vols.), and *Ethics* (2 vols.).

7. Later, in the revolution of 1911, Ch'en Ch'i-mei seized Shanghai for the revolutionists and became its military governor. The uncle of Ch'en Kuo-fu, he was also senior commander in the revolutionary army, where Chiang Kai-shek served.

Chapter Four

1. This article, which was discovered after the publication of *MSCC* in 1928, can be found in *Man-shu ta-shih chi-nien chi (A Memorial Volume of the Reverend Man-shu's Works),* edited by Liu Wu-chi (Chungking, 1943), pp. 147–52; the quotation is from p. 152.

2. In his letter to Liu San (October 11, 1908), Man-shu was misled by hearsay into stating that Yang was "an old man of more than eighty."

For an account of Yang Wen-hui and his family in Nanking, see Yang Pu-wei (Mrs. Y. R. Chao), *The Autobiography of a Chinese Woman* (Chinese ed.), Taipei, 1967, pp. 83–98. Mrs. Y.R. Chao, the author of a famous Chinese cookbook, is Yang Wen-hui's granddaughter. She and Professor Y. R. Chao, an internationally known Chinese linguist, are now living in the United States.

3. See Otto Franke, "Ein Buddhistischer Reformversuch in China" in *T'oung Pao*, Serie II, Bd. X (1909), 567–602. Best known as an historian, Franke was interested in the influence of Buddhism on China and published from 1907 to 1910 the following articles (in addition to the one mentioned above): "Japans Buddhistische Propaganda in China" (1907), "Die Ausbreitung des Buddhismus von Indien nach Turkistan und China" (1909), and "Zur Frage der Einführung des Buddhismus in China" (1910).

4. The date of its publication could not be earlier than October, 1909, as it contains Fletcher's preface, dated October 6. Also, in his poem to Man-shu in September, 1909, Liu San referred to "the patriotic poems of Byron" as "Man-shu's new translation, which he planned to publish soon."

5. "Lien-hua," is lotus or waterlily. In this case, it seems to be Man-shu's translation of the lady's first name, more properly "Lily" than "Lotus."

6. The expression, *hsiao-chia pi-yü* (literally, "small-family," "green-jade"), means "a pretty girl from a humble family."

Chapter Five

1. Poets who flourished during the reigns of the T'ung-ch'ih and Kuang-hsü emperors (1862–1907). Their later representatives were Ch'en San-li (a sponsor of the Jetavana School) and Cheng Hsiao-hsü (later prime minister of the Japanese puppet Manchukuo regime).

2. The Administrative *Yüan*, Wang Chao-ming (Wang Ching-wei); the Legislative *Yüan*, Shao Yüan-ch'ung and Yeh Ch'u-ts'ang; the Judicial *Yüan*, Chang Chi and Chü Cheng; the Examination *Yüan*, Tai Chi-t'ao; the Control *Yüan*, Yü Yu-jen. The last three were presidents of their respective *yüan* for almost twenty years each. Wang Chao-ming's political career came to a tragic end when he bolted the Nationalist party to become the head of the puppet Nanking regime under Japanese occupation. While Shao Yüan-ch'ung had only a short term as vice president and acting president of the Legislative *Yüan*, its vice presidency was held later by Yeh Ch'u-ts'ang, who was concurrently secretary general of the Nationalist party's Central Executive Committee.

3. In the first volume of the *Journal of Southern Society* (January, 1910), six of Su Man-shu's poems are included in the "Poetry Section," edited by Kao T'ien-mei.

4. Lin Shu (1852–1924) and Yen Fu (1853–1921) were two of the best known early translators of Western works; Lin Shu was especially noted for his translations of fiction. *Hototogisu* (1900), a novel by Tokutomi

Roka (Tokutomi Kenjiro, 1868–1927), was translated into English as *Nami-ko* in 1905. Ku Hung-ming (1857–1928), a noted Confucian scholar and monarchist, was known to the West mainly for his rendering of the *Four Confucian Books* into English. When William Cowper heard the story of John Gilpin from Lady Austen, he lay awake at night laughing over it and then made a ballad of it, of which the first line of the last stanza reads "Now, let us sing—Long live the king." It took Ts'ao Chih (192–232) seven steps to compose a poem in which to attack his elder brother, the emperor.

5. In the first part of the same letter, he told Kao and Liu of a new attack of consumption, which cost him more than $700 during his six months' stay on the island.

6. Henry McAleavy, *op. cit.,* pp. 12–16.

7. To my knowledge, there is no record of the publication in Europe of any English translation of this famous Chinese play. An inquiry by Lo Hsiao-ming to the Biblioteca Nacional at Madrid in 1967 brought an anticipated negative reply from its director.

8. McAleavy has argued very convincingly against the possibility of (1) a Spaniard's teaching English in Hong Kong; (2) the marriage offer by Señor Lopez; (3) his financing Man-shu's education in the Buddhist doctrine (*op. cit.,* p. 15).

Chapter Six

1. "To" is a bell with a clapper. It is said in the Confucian *Analects:* "Heaven is about to use the Master as a bell with a wooden clapper"—i.e., to arouse the age.

2. "Shen-chou," literally "Divine State," is a name for China.

3. "Min-kuo," here translated literally, means "republican."

4. A short preface to the poem reads as follows: "After having packed my luggage for a homeward trip to visit my mother, I was about to leave Java when I ran into my old friend Chang Yün-lei, also on his way back to China. Deeply affected by the meeting, I wrote this poem." Fan P'ang and Chang Chien were both scholar-officials of the second century A.D., who had offended and suffered from the persecutions of the powerful eunuchs at court. Before Fan P'ang was executed, he bade farewell to his aged mother, regretting that he had failed to give her comfort in her old age. Chang Chien, slightly later, went from house to house to escape arrest by the eunuchs.

5. "But the story that by the age of nineteen he was already such a competent scholar of Sanskrit that he had made for Chinese a grammar of that language is totally incredible, and indeed when we consider the way in which he passed his life it is hard to imagine that he can at any time have acquired more than a smattering of Sanskrit." McAleavy, *op. cit.,* p. 15. It is to be noted here that Man-shu was twenty-three, not nineteen,

when he compiled the *Sanskrit Grammar*. McAleavy, who got this "story" from Liu Wu-chi's "Chronological Life of Su Man-shu" (published in 1927), apparently failed to see a revised version of the same work (published a year later in the *Complete Works of Man-shu*, IV, 303–53), in which many changes were made, including a revision of the date of the *Sanskrit Grammar*.

6. This happened to Liu Ya-tzu and Liu Wu-chi when they first attempted to reconstruct Man-shu's life from the "Postscript." At that time they had to start from scratch, there being little material (beyond a few letters, poems, essays) on which to build a chronology of Man-shu's life. It was not until several years later that Liu Ya-tzu was able to collect, through his painstaking efforts and with the help of Man-shu's friends and relatives, enough firsthand material to rewrite the biography and finalize the "Chronological Life."

7. See Chapter Two, p. 36 for the reason of Man-shu's sudden decision to become a Buddhist monk.

8. This Buddhist certificate, which belonged originally to the real Po-ching, a monk from the family of Chao in Shih-hsing county, Nan-hsiung prefecture, was found among Man-shu's belongings after his death. It was reproduced in *Man-shu's Literary Remains*, published by Liu Ya-tzu in 1929.

9. Even then, several cousins and nephews mentioned in his letters and diaries cannot be identified or placed in this table. They were probably the sons and grandsons of Su Chieh-sheng's younger brothers born by Jung-shih, Su Chieh-sheng's father's concubine.

10. The argument here is that Su Hsü-t'ing, although already ten years old in 1884, was at the Su family home in Li-ch'i and therefore unaware of the circumstances surrounding his brother's birth in faraway Japan. On the other hand, Elder Ch'en-shih, who was with Su Chieh-sheng at his Yokohama home, was naturally privy to this affair.

Chapter Seven

1. See pp. 74–75.

2. In another passage in the *Random Notes*, Man-shu tells us about the many kinds of lotus flowers in India. Not only are there pink and white lotus flowers, but also gold, yellow, blue, and purple ones.

3. The reference to Central India is not clear. So far as is known, Man-shu never set foot in India, though he probably went to Ceylon during his southern trip in 1904.

4. A monastery outside Soochow where the famous T'ang monk Han Shan (Cold Mountain) lived.

5. A poem in the *Ch'u Tz'u* anthology, sometimes attributed to the Ch'u poet, Ch'ü Yüan.

6. A reference to the lady in the moon.

7. Given him by Ch'iu-yün with a piece of jade. He sold the jade but apparently kept the crimson kerchief all this time.

8. Man-shu must have met Chiang Kai-shek in Japan between 1913 and 1916, but there is no other evidence of their friendship besides this recollection by Ch'en Kuo-fu.

9. Previously in December, 1916, while in Hangchow, Man-shu had worked on another story, the "Tale of a Man and a Ghost," but only a little over one thousand words were written down and the manuscript has not survived.

Chapter Eight

1. Pei-hsin also published the works of some well-known writers of the New Literature Movement, such as the brothers Chou Shu-jen (Lu Hsün) and Chou Tso-jen.

2. Because of its size, eighteen hundred pages in five volumes, the Pei-hsin *Complete Works of Man-shu,* which has long been out of print, most likely will not soon be reissued. On the market today are several reprints of other editions, of which the best is the *Complete Works of the Reverend Man-shu,* originally published in 1934 in Shanghai, and edited by Wen Kung-chih. Wen's edition contains some of the new materials discovered by Liu Ya-tzu too late for inclusion in the Pei-hsin volumes, but it is marred by a number of inaccuracies and the inclusion of some materials wrongly attributed to Man-shu as a result of a desire to make the edition "the most complete." Other important editions of Man-shu's works include a popular edition of the *Complete Works of Su Man-shu,* edited by Liu Ya-tzu and published by the K'ai-hua Book Company in Shanghai in 1933, and *A Memorial Volume of the Reverend Man-shu's Works,* edited by Liu Wu-chi and published by the Cheng-feng Press, Chungking, in 1943 on the twenty-fifth anniversary of Man-shu's death. Both books are out of print.

3. Paraphrased from a statement in Liu Wu-chi, "A Note on *Two Newly Discovered Works Written by Man-shu*" (1927), in Liu Ya-tzu, *MSCC,* IV, 107–10.

4. This statement, which occurs twice in "Tale of a Broken Hairpin," is omitted in McAleavy's English translation (*Su Man-shu, A Sino-Japanese Genius,* pp. 38–48).

5. A popular Japanese cold drink; the ice is usually flavored.

6. Chang Ping-lin, "Foreword" to Ts'ai Shou's edition of Man-shu's paintings, included in Liu Ya'tzu, *op. cit.,* IV, 77–78.

7. *Ibid.,* IV, 82. Although Liu Ya-tzu's preface is dated October 8, 1918, this first anthology of Man-shu's poetry, edited by Huang Tê-chung and published by Liu Ya-tzu, did not appear until a year or two later.

8. *Ibid.,* IV, 141.

9. *Ibid.*, IV, 80.

10. Chang Ping-lin was referring to the time when Man-shu was with him and Liu Shih-p'ei in Japan in 1907. Apparently he did not believe, as some have claimed, that Man-shu joined Sun Yat-sen's China Revolutionary Party in 1914. We tend to agree with Chang.

11. Chang Ping-lin, "Notes on Su Man-shu's Life," in Liu Ya-tzu, *op. cit.*, IV, 134–35.

12. Quoted by Liu Wu-chi in his "Chronological Life of Su Man-shu," in Liu Ya-tzu, *op. cit.*, IV, 337–38.

13. Liu Ya-tzu, *op. cit.*, IV, 24.

14. These related to the Han and T'ang periods; he copied illustrations from books in libraries in Japan. Liu Ya-tzu once had in his possession some of these pencil sketches, but the manuscript is lost.

15. Literally, "the seed-case of the lotus sticking aslant." Here, I take to mean a woman's hairknot shaped like a lotus seedcase. It is more likely for a girl to have this kind of hairdo than for her to stick a lotus seedcase in her hair, which would make her look rather grotesque, instead of pretty.

16. Literally, "peach-blossom cheeks and sandalwood mouth." The first is the equivalent of "rosy cheeks" in English and the second refers to the fragrance of the sandalwood.

17. The original expression is *t'ou-k'ou,* meaning nutmeg and its flower.

18. Yü Ta-fu's article is included in Liu Ya-tzu, *op. cit.*, V, 114–25; this particular quotation appears in V, 119. A member of the Creation Society, Yü Ta-fu was himself a prolific writer of fiction in the third decade of the twentieth century.

19. McAleavy, *op. cit.*, p. 38.

20. Hu Shih, *Collections of Hu Shih's Literary Writings,* (Taipei, 1953), I, 43. *Strange Stories from a Chinese Studio,* a collection of ghost and animal spirit stories by P'u Sung-ling, a seventeenth-century writer, has been partially translated into English by Herbert A. Giles.

21. Yü Ta-fu, "Miscellaneous Criticism of Man-shu's Writings," in Liu Ya-tzu, *op. cit.*, V, 115–16. Hu Shih's article, written in 1922, can be found in Hu Shih, *op. cit.*, II, 180–260.

22. Chou Tso-jen, "A Letter in Reply to Mr. Yün-shen," May 30, 1927, in Liu Ya-tzu, *op. cit.*, V, 127.

23. *Ibid.*, V, 128. Chou Tso-jen is the only writer to have regarded Man-shu as a major figure in the "Mandarin Duck and Butterfly School." While Man-shu was active during the same period this school of fiction was flourishing (1908–18), and was associated with its leading writers (some were also members of the Southern Society), critics generally believed that Man-shu was outside their inner circle and that his writings differ from theirs. Scholars on mainland China today consider Pao T'ien-hsiao as the leader of this school, which has taken on a derogatory sense, and Pao himself has denied this allegation (1960). For a study of this school

of fiction—the origin of its name, lists of its writers and their works, excerpts of critical opinions on it—see Wei Shao-ch'ang (ed.), *Research Materials on the Mandarin Duck and Butterfly School*, Shanghai, 1962.

24. Liu Ya-tzu, "The Problem of Man-shu's Buddhist Certificate," in Liu Wu-chi (ed.), *A Memorial Volume of the Reverend Man-shu's Works*, (Appendix), pp. 493–96.

25. Although Su Shao-ch'iung killed herself by drinking poison during a quarrel with her parents over an alleged love affair with a school teacher, she left behind, it is said, a copy of Man-shu's works on her deathbed. She herself had written two poems in memory of Man-shu:

Poet, you wandering poet,
I, your niece, have seen you in a vision,
Wearing your "straw-sandals" and holding your "broken alms-bowl,"
As you roamed the "cherry-blossom bridges."

Poet, you wandering poet,
It also seems that I have seen you,
Wearing your cassock and holding a volume of your poems,
As you chanted them on the Orphan Hill.
You, Orphan Hill, so lonely,
Are a fit companion for the poet, Man-shu.

See Huang Min-ch'i, *A Critical Biography of Su Man-shu* (Shanghai, 1949) pp. 61–62.

26. For comment on Wen's edition, see note 2 to this chapter.

27. The book contains a reprint of Liu Wu-chi's "A Chronological Life of Su Man-shu" (from the 1928 Pei-hsin *Complete Works*), in which the author's name is abbreviated as "Liu Wu."

28. Lin Hsi (the pseudonym of Kao Pai-yü), in "Constellation," *The Singapore Daily*, October 13, 1965.

29. As of 1970, these four are (1) Pao T'ien-hsiao, age ninety-six; (2) Chang Shih-chao, age ninety; (3) Ch'en Kuo-ch'üan, age eighty-two; (4) Shen Yen-mou, age eighty. Shen died on June 28, 1971.

30. This "Poetry Album" was formerly in the possession of Chang Ch'ing-ch'eng, the widow of Ts'ai Shou, Man-shu's good friend and a member of the Southern Society. Its present owner, who showed it to Kao Pai-yü, is given in the article as a Mr. Lo. The album contains twenty-three poems by Man-shu (all in his fine handwriting and mostly on Japanese stationery), four translated poems by Man-shu, ten poems by Ch'en Tu-hsiu, and one poem by Teng Sheng-hou. Apparently, the authenticity of the album is not questioned by Pao T'ien-hsiao and Chang Shih-chao. Unfortunately, it has not been possible to examine the album or to secure a reproduction.

31. Much of the information in this paragraph is supplied by Lo Hsiao-ming, who has been in correspondence with Iizuka Akira about Su Man-shu. An interesting article by Iizuka Akira is entitled "Su Man-shu and the heroine, Sakuntala" (1947).

32. "Poets and Poetry of China's Last Empire," *Literature, East and West,* IX (December, 1965), 331–61.

33. *Ibid.*, p. 359.

34. Not a new biography, but a reprint of Feng Tzu-yu's article, "True Facts of Man-shu's Life," much used by McAleavy in his account of Man-shu's early life.

35. "A Revolutionary Literary Organization—the Southern Society" in *A History of Chinese Literature* (Peking, 1958), II, 671–75; "The Revolution-Promoting Southern Society" in *A History of Chinese Literature* (Shanghai, 1959), III, 487–95.

36. *A History of Chinese Literature* (Shanghai, 1959), III, 494–95.

Selected Bibliography

PRIMARY SOURCES

Man-shu ch'üan-chi (Complete Works of Man-shu), ed. by Liu Ya-tzu and Liu Wu-chi. 5 vols. Shanghai: Pei-hsin Book Co., 1928. Standard edition; useful materials on his life.

Man-shu ta-shih chi-nien chi (A Memorial Volume of the Reverend Man-shu's Works), ed. by Liu Wu-chi. Chungking: Cheng-feng Press, 1943. A reprint of Man-shu's works, commemorating the twenty-fifth anniversary of his death.

Man-shu ta-shih ch'üan-chi (Complete Works of the Reverend Man-shu), ed. by Wen Kung-chih. Shanghai:Yu-i Book Co., 1934. Reprinted, Hong Kong: Wen-yüan Book Co. (n.d.). Best available edition.

SECONDARY SOURCES

1. Chinese and Japanese Books

CHANG PING-LIN. *T'ai-yen hsien-sheng tzu-t'ing nien-p'u* (A Chronological Autobiography of Chang T'ai-yen). Hong Kong: Lung-meng Book Co., 1965. The best source on the early years of Chang Ping-lin's life, during which time he was engaged in revolutionary activities.

CHIANG I-AN. *Man-shu shih yü ni Man-shu shih* (Man-shu's Poems and Imitations of Man-shu's Poems). Taipei: Commercial Press, 1965. A volume of Man-shu's poems and Chiang's imitations, showing the influence of the former on recent writers.

Chung-kuo hsiao-shuo shih kao (A History of Chinese Fiction, First Draft), compiled by the Editorial Committee on the History of Chinese Fiction, class of 1955, Chinese Department, National Peking University. Peking: Jen-min wen-hsüeh Press, 1960. This latest history of Chinese fiction from mainland China contains critical notice of Man-shu's novels and stories. It indicates acceptance by contemporary Chinese critics of his position as a novelist, some forty years after his death.

Chung-kuo wen-hsüeh shih (A History of Chinese Literature), compiled by the Classical Literature Section, Chinese Department, Futan University. 3 vols. Shanghai: Chung-hua Book Co., 1959. A section on the

Southern Society as a revolutionary literary organization in the early 1900's mentions Su Man-shu and Liu Ya-tzu as its representative writers. (III, 487–495).

FENG TZU-YU. *Ko-ming i-shih* (Anecdotes of the Chinese Revolution). 5 vols. Taipei: Commercial Press, (2nd ed.), 1965. Most important background material on the history of the pre-1911 revolutions, including personal reminiscences of Man-shu and his many friends of the early revolutionary period.

HUANG MING-CH'I. *Su Man-shu p'ing-chuan* (A Critical Biography of Su Man-shu). Shanghai: Pai-hsin Book Co., 1949. The only book-length biography of Man-shu in Chinese, based upon materials found in the writings of Liu Ya-tzu and Liu Wu-chi.

KURATA SADAYOSHI. *Chugoku kindai shi no kenkyu* (A Study of Modern Chinese Poetry). Tokyo: Taishu kan shoten, 1969. A recent study of Chinese poetry of late Ch'ing and early Republican period with a detailed account of the Southern Society poets, including Su Man-shu and Liu Ya-tzu.

LIU WU-CHI. *Su Man-shu nien-p'u chi ch'i-t'a* (A Chronological Life of Su Man-shu and Other Articles). Shanghai: Pei-hsin Book Co., 1927. First attempt at a systematic study and presentation of Man-shu's life; some errors.

LIU YA-TZU. *Nan-shê chi-lüeh* (A Brief Account of the Southern Society). Shanghai: K'ai-hua Book Co., 1940. An authoritative, though brief, account of this revolutionary literary organization by one of its founders.

SATÔ HARUO. "So Man-ju to wa ikanam hito zo" ("What Kind of Person is Su Man-shu?"), in *Karamono Innen*, pp. 14–28. Tokyo: Keisō shobō, 1965. An example of Japanese interest in Su Man-shu.

Shang-hai-shih t'ung-chih-kuan ch'i-k'an (Journal of the Gazetteer Bureau of Shanghai). Vol. I (June, 1933–March, 1934); Vol. II (June, 1934–March, 1935). Reprinted, Hong Kong: Lung-meng Book Co., 1965. Several articles on literary organizations in Shanghai, including the Southern Society, in the first decades of the twentieth century.

Ta-t'ung hsüeh-hsiao lüeh-shih (A Brief History of the Ta-t'ung School). Yokohama, 1909. Only source material on this first important Chinese school established by the Chinese community in Yokohama. A unique copy of this work is in Lo Hsiao-ming's possession.

Yüan-yang hu-tieh p'ai yen-chiu tzu-liao (Research Materials on the Mandarin-Duck and Butterfly School), ed. by Wei Shao-ch'ang. Shanghai: Wen-i Press, 1962. A collection of articles on this school of Chinese fiction popular in the 1910's and 1920's.

2. Chinese Periodicals

Chia-yen tsa-chih (The Tiger). Shanghai and Tokyo, Vol. I, nos. 1–10 (1914–15). A literary and political monthly edited by Chang Shih-chao and containing poems and stories by Man-shu, prefaces to the stories, and his friends' poems to him.

Hsin ch'ing-nien tsa-chih (*La Jeunesse*). Shanghai, Vol. II, nos. 3–4 (November–December, 1916); Vol. V, no. 6 (December, 1918). A literary and political monthly founded by Ch'en Tu-hsiu, containing a story by Man-shu; also condolences on Man-shu's death by his friends.

Kuo-min jih-jih pao (National People's Daily; The China National Gazette). Shanghai, August–December, 1903; *Kuo-min jih-jih pao hui-pien* (National People's Daily, Newly Collected and Compiled). Shanghai, 1904. 4 vols. Reprinted (August 8—August 23; September 21—October 19, 1903). Taipei: Taiwan Hsüeh-sheng Book Co., 1965. A radical revolutionary daily registered under A. Gomoll and edited by Chang Shih-chao, Ch'en Tu-hsiu, and others; one of the earliest newspapers in Shanghai. Man-shu's contributions include a few poems, two articles, and an unfinished translation of Hugo's *Les Misérables*.

Kuo-ts'ui hsüeh-pao (Journal of the Nation's Essential Cultural Heritage). Shanghai, Nos. 1–82 (1905–11). A learned literary monthly edited by Teng Shih and Huang Chieh; it contains records of the books Man-shu donated to the library of the association which published the journal.

Min-kuo tsa-chih (The Republic). Tokyo, Nos. 1–6 (1914). A political publication, monthly organ of Sun Yat-sen's Kuomintang (Nationalist party), then in exile in Japan, edited by Hu Han-min, Tai Chi-t'ao, and others. It contains important contributions, including poems, essays, and an incomplete novel by Man-shu in the later part of his life.

Min-pao (People's Report; The Minpao Magazine). Tokyo, Nos. 1–24 (October, 1905–October, 1908); Paris, Nos. 24–25 (1910). Reprinted, Peking K'o-hsüeh Press, 1957. Political organ of Sun Yat-sen's Chinese Revolutionary party, monthly (irregular), edited by Chang Chi, Chang Ping-lin, Wang Chao-ming (editor of the last two issues, published clandestinely in Tokyo, not in Paris, as indicated on the cover), and others. Man-shu knew the editors and stayed with Chang Ping-lin in his office for some time in his early year in Japan.

T'ien-i pao (Tien Yee News). Tokyo, Nos. 1–19 (June, 1907–March, 1908). Reprint (incomplete), Tokyo: Daian, 1966. A semimonthly; first Chinese periodical devoted to the propagation of Anarchist and Socialist ideas, edited by Liu Shih-p'ei and his wife, Ho Cheng, with whom Man-shu stayed after moving out from the *Min-pao* office.

3. Western-Language Books and Articles

FRANKE, OTTO. "Ein buddhistischer Reformversuch in China," in *T'oung Pao*, Serie II, Bd. X (1909), 567–602. A detailed account of the Buddhist reform movement led by Yang Jen-shan, whom the author visited in Nanking in 1908.

LEUNG, GEORGE KIN, tr. *The Lone Swan.* Shanghai: Commercial Press, 1924. Reprinted, Hong Kong: Li-sheng Book Co., 1961.

MC ALEAVY, HENRY. *Su Man-shu, A Sino-Japanese Genius.* (China Society Sinological Series, No. 6) London: China Society, 1960. The only previous study in English of Man-shu's life based upon accounts by Feng Tzu-yu and others, including partial translations of *The Lone Swan* and "Tale of a Broken Hairpin."

WONG, RAMON and IRVING Y. C. LO. "Poets and Poetry of China's Last Empire," in *Literature: East and West*, IX (December, 1965), 331–61. Man-shu is included among late Ch'ing poets in this survey.

Appendix I. A Genealogy of the Su Clan

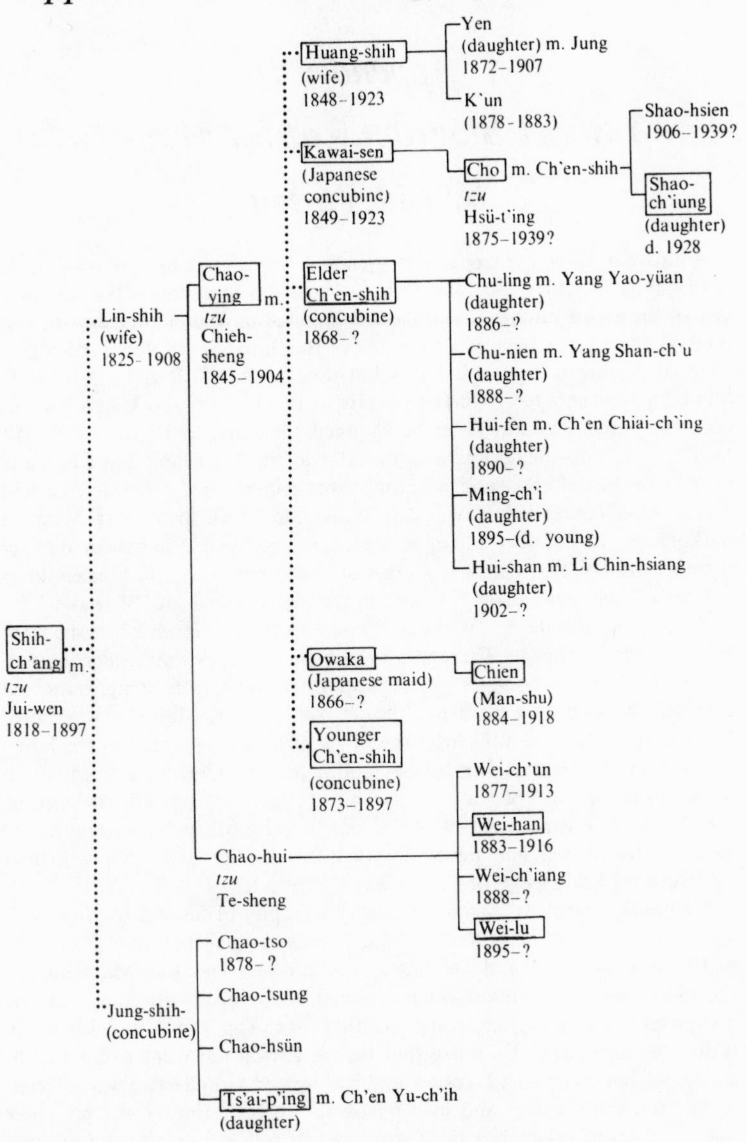

* Names in rectangles are those mentioned in the biography.

Appendix II
A Short Biography of Su Man-shu by Liu Ya-tzu

A native of Li-ch'i village in Kung-ch'ang township, Chung-shan county, Kwangtung province, Su Man-shu was born on September 28 (the tenth day of the eighth month, lunar calendar), 1884 in Yokohama, Japan, and died on May 2 (the twenty-second day of the third month, lunar calendar), 1918 at Kuang-tz'u Hospital in Chin-shen-fu Road [Rue Père Robert], Shanghai, at the age of thirty-five. His original name was Chien and his courtesy name, Tzu-ku. Later he changed his name to Hsüan-ying.[1] His father, Su Chieh-sheng, was a comprador at the Wan-lung Tea Company in Yokohama. He had one wife and three concubines, of whom the first was a Japanese called Kawai-sen. When Su Chieh-sheng was living in Yokohama, he hired a Japanese maid-servant, whose name no one remembers today but who was known at that time in the Su household as "Owaka." It is said that "Owaka" is the abbreviation of "Wakako-san" and her name should be "Wakako." She was only nineteen when she went to Chieh-sheng's house. There was a red mole on her bosom, which according to the Chinese book of physiognomy, so said Chieh-sheng, indicated that she "should give birth to a noble son." Later, Man-shu was born. But less than three months after the boy's birth, she returned to her home and no one knew anything further about her. So Chieh-sheng entrusted Man-shu to the care of Kawai-sen, who brought him up. Throughout his life, Man-shu regarded Kawai-sen as his blood mother. According to my surmise, Kawai-sen had never revealed this fact to Man-shu, who had therefore no knowledge of the "Owaka" episode.

Previously, when we wrote "A New Biography of Su Hsüan-ying" and "A Chronological Life of Su Man-shu," we were misled by the "Postscript to *Voices of the Tide*" and *The Lone Swan* into believing that Man-shu was the blood son of a Japanese man named Mūne-o, an allegation that is completely wrong. I feel, however, that Man-shu did not deliberately falsify his parentage. He knew that before Kawai-sen went to Su Chieh-sheng, she had married a Japanese and had by him a child (who was referred to in Man-shu's letters and in a postscript to his painting as "my elder sister, Enomoto Eiko). For this reason he was rather suspicious of his own

[1] He also took the Buddhist name, Man-shu, by which he is known to posterity.

consanguinity. So doubts led to conjecture, which resulted in the compilation of the "Postscript to *Voices of the Tide*" and *The Lone Swan*. In the end, as he himself could not verify his conjecture, he did not include the "Postscript" in *Voices of the Tide* when it was printed, but had little scruple in publishing *The Lone Swan*, which is after all a work of fiction. This also explains his constant reference to the unutterable pangs of his life. Now, from my correspondence with Man-shu's cousin, Su Wei-lu, who heard it from Elder Ch'en-shih, Chieh-sheng's second concubine and an eyewitness to the affair at that time, we learn that Man-shu was not the blood son of Kawai-sen and so the question of the "oil jar"[2] need not deter us here. Thus the case of Man-shu's blood kinship can be said to be completely solved.

At age six (1889), Man-shu returned to Li-ch'i with Huang-shih, Chieh-sheng's legal wife; at seven, he studied at a village school. When Man-shu was nine, Chieh-sheng, who had failed in his business in Yokohama, returned to Li-ch'i with his second concubine, Elder Ch'en-shih. After having stayed home for three years, Chieh-sheng left for Shanghai with her but did not take Man-shu along. It was not until 1896 that Man-shu went to Shanghai with his paternal aunt to live together with Chieh-sheng and Elder Ch'en-shih. There he started to learn English. In 1897 Chieh-sheng returned to Li-ch'i on account of his father's illness and when the latter died, Elder Ch'en-shih too left Shanghai, leaving Man-shu at his aunt's house. A year later (1898) Man-shu was taken by Lin Tzu-yüan, his elder cousin [his paternal grandmother's brother's grandson] to Yokohama, where he entered Ta-t'ung School founded by the Chinese communities there. After his graduation in 1902 he went to Tokyo to enroll in the Senior Preparatory Course at Waseda University and a year later (1903) transferred to Ch'eng-ch'eng Military Academy [Seizo Gakko]. He joined the Anti-Russian Volunteer Corps and the Association for the People's Military Education. By that time Man-shu's revolutionary thoughts had gradually matured but Lin Tzu-yüan was opposed to Man-shu's participation in the revolution and cut off his school allowance to force him to return to Kwangtung. Who would have thought that as soon as Man-shu reached Shanghai, he landed and then sent to Tzu-yüan a letter, saying that he was going to drown himself in the sea! There was very little that Tzu-yüan could do. From Shanghai Man-shu proceeded to Soochow and taught at the Soochow Community School. Later he returned to Shanghai to work as a translator for the *National People's Daily*. One day, soon after the paper had folded, he beguiled Ch'en Tu-hsiu, Chang Hsing-yen, [Chang Shih-chao] and Ho Mei-shih by taking them to a theater and then returning to their lodging, made off with some thirty dollars that belonged

[2] A Chinese colloquial expression, meaning the child of a woman by her first husband.

to Chang Hsing-yen. Right away he slipped to Hong Kong, where he stayed at the office of *The China Daily*. Still he was not happy with his life there and conceived the idea of leaving this world. So he went from Hong Kong to a dilapidated temple at Hui-chou. There he presented himself to a Buddhist master and shaved his head to become a novice. He was not used, however, to the rigors of monastic life and one day, when his teacher went away to beg for alms, he stole the Buddhist certificate of a fellow monk and departed. This fellow monk, who had recently passed away, came from the family of Chao in Shih-hsing county in Nan-hsiung prefecture; he was ordained at Hui-lung Monastery in Hsin-hui and given a religious name, Po-ching, and a spiritual name, Ch'ao-fan. After Man-shu had come into possession of this certificate, he henceforth styled himself Po-ching, a devotee of Hui-lung Monastery. In the first month of the lunar calendar, 1904, he returned to Hong Kong. One day he happened to meet Chien Shih-ch'ang, a villager from Chung-shan. When the latter went back, he told Chieh-sheng about the encounter. At that time, Chieh-sheng was already seriously ill; so he sent Chien Shih-ch'ang back to Hong Kong to persuade Man-shu to return home so that he could attend to his father's last hours. Man-shu, who had shown little affection for Chieh-sheng, was especially displeased with him for his severance of marital relationship with Kawai-sen at Elder Ch'en-shih's instigation. So he told Chien Shih-ch'ang: "I'm just a penniless tramp. What's the use of my going home?" There was little that Chien Shih-ch'ang could do but to return without accomplishing the mission. A few days later, Chieh-sheng died. Thus completely severing himself from the Su family, Man-shu started his wandering life at the age of twenty-one. According to Ch'eng Yen-sheng, however, Man-shu got some money from the younger brother of Huang-shih, Chieh-sheng's legal wife, for his trip to Ceylon, but this statement still needs verification.

When Man-shu arrived at Shanghai from Hong Kong he decided to take a trip southward and subsequently visited Siam, Ceylon, and other places. While there, he began to learn Sanskrit. Not long afterwards, he returned to China to engage in a teaching career. He went to Ch'ang-sha twice to teach respectively at the Industrial School and Ming-tê School; to Nanking at the Elementary Military School; to Wu-hu at Wan-chiang School. In 1907 he went to Japan where he worked with Chang T'ai-yen [Chang Ping-lin] for the *People's Report* [*Min-pao*] and with Liu Shen-shu [Liu Shih-p'ei] for the *Tien Yee News* [*T'ien-i-pao*]. The former was an organ of the China Alliance [Chung-kuo t'ung-meng hui] which aimed to foment national revolution while the latter advocated anarchism. The next year (1908) he went again to Nanking to help Yang Jen-shan [Yang Wen-hui] in establishing the Jetavana Institute [Chih-yüan ching-shê]. In 1909 he went to Southeast Asia for the second time—first to Singapore and later to Surabaya in Java, where he stayed to teach at the China Guild House

[Chung-hua hui-kuan]. During this period, Man-shu clamored everyday for a trip to India but was not able to make it. He returned to Japan during the summer vacation of 1911 and went back to Surabaya in the fall. On October 10th (the 19th day of the eighth month, lunar calendar) of the same year, the Revolutionary Army revolted in Wu-ch'ang. Man-shu was greatly excited by the event but could not raise enough money for the voyage homeward and had to spend the New Year's Eve at Surabaya. In the second month of the lunar calendar, 1912, he returned to Shanghai but when he discovered that the situation in the country was still hopeless, he could only hide himself in the houses of pleasure to indulge day after day in the feast of "flowers and wine."[3] It was then that he published in *The Pacific News* [*T'ai-p'ing-yang pao*] the novel *The Lone Swan.*

In the winter of 1912, Man-shu taught at the Anhwei High School in An-ch'ing but left it before the summer vacation of 1913. After having wandered about for several months between Soochow and Hangchow and having stayed for sometime in Shanghai at the Number One Hotel on Nanking Road, he returned once again to his home in Japan. As a son, Man-shu cherished great affection for Kawai-sen and went frequently to Japan to see her. This time he dwelled there for two whole years from 1914 through 1915. By then, the Nationalist Party [Kuomintang] had been defeated and many of its important members were living in Japan. Man-shu was thus on friendly terms with Sun Chung-san [Sun Yat-sen] as well as with Hsiao Jen-ch'iu, Yang Ts'ang-pai, Chü Chio-sheng [Chü Cheng], Shao Yüan-ch'ung, Teng Meng-shih, T'ien Tzu-ch'in [T'ien T'ung], and Tai Chi-t'ao. He published in *The Republic* [*Min kuo tsa-chih*], the Party organ, an incomplete story and some miscellaneous writings. Later Man-shu also contributed to *The Tiger* [*Chia-yen*] published by Chang Hsing-yen, and *La Jeunesse* [*Hsin-ch'ing-nien*] by Ch'en Tu-hsiu. In 1916 he returned to China; the next year, in the intercalary second month of the lunar calendar, he took another trip to Japan but hastened back soon afterwards. During this period Man-shu already suffered from frequent attacks of acute stomach ailment, which prevented him from making further trips to Japan. In the fall of that year, he stayed in Shanghai with Chiang Chung-cheng [Chiang Kai-shek] and Ch'en Kuo-fu at 11 Hsin-min Lane, Pai-erh-pu Road [Rue Eugene Bard]; the same winter he entered Hai-ning Hospital but failed to receive adequate treatment. In spring, 1918, he moved to Kuang-tz'u Hospital, where he died of sickness. Thus passed away this genius of our age as he cast off the burdens of this filthy world.

Man-shu was neither systematic nor salutary in his thoughts but in literature and the arts he had talents that cannot be obliterated. At present, a certain group of young men worship him with a mad zeal while not a few

[3] I.e., in the company of sing-song girls.

others are dissatisfied with him. Anyway, I feel it will not be fair to wipe away Man-shu's name from any history of Chinese literature if it is to be a complete and comprehensive one.[4]

[4] The last part of this biography, which gives detailed lists of Man-shu's works and later publications on him, as well as information on members of Man-shu's family and their relations to him, is omitted here.

Index

Account of My Refugee Life on the Seashores of Sala (An), 53, 55–56, 62, 125
"Admonishment to All Buddhist Disciples" (An), 58–59, 124
Affinities in Literature, 56–58, 62, 80, 110, 123, 141
Ai-kuo hsüeh-shê (see Patriotic Student Society)
"Alas! We Cantonese!", 32–33
Amoy University, 90
An-ch'ing, 97–98, 129
"Anecdotes of the Reverend Man-shu," 126
Anhwei, 25, 41–42
Anhwei High School, 97–99, 129
Annam, 39
Army Elementary School, 41–42
Asoka (King), 57
Association for Asian Studies, 140
Association for the People's Military Education, 28–29
Association for the Preservation of National Learning, 38, 50
"Autumn Night" (The), 98
Awakening of Faith in the Mahayana Doctrine (The), 60

"Ballad of Mu-lan," 56
Bangkok, 39
Berlin University, 60
Bharata, King, 62
"Bidding Farewell to T'ang Kuo-tun with Two Poems and a Painting," 30, 32
Biographies of the Revolutionary Martyrs and Early Revolutionists, 141
Biwa, Lake, 66
Bodhi Temple, 39
Botanic Treatise on the Flora of the Western Hemisphere (A), 79
Boxers, 24–25
British in Hong Kong, 33; in India, 55–56, 124; in Shanghai, 19, 32
Buddha, 57, 64, 72, 79–80, 120, 134
Buddhism, 32, 36–37, 39–40, 46–47, 58–61, 66, 75–79, 87, 91–95, 105, 107–8, 111–12, 119, 124, 127, 134–35, 142
Buddhist Institute (see Jetavana School)
Buffalo, New York, 32
Bungei Shunju, 139
Burma, 100–101
Burns, 81, 100
Byron, 51, 57, 62–64, 73, 80, 82, 94, 96, 100, 108, 124, 133, 140

Candlin, Clara, 57, 78
Candlin, Rev. George, 56–57, 78, 124
Canton, 41–42, 68, 80, 83, 87
Ceylon, 39, 78, 80, 100
Chang Chi, 27, 31–32, 44–45
Chang Chien, 85
Chang Chüan-chüan, 106
Chang Ping-lin, 25–26, 31–32, 37, 43, 45–48, 50, 52–53, 57–59, 61–62, 64, 74–75, 84, 87, 98, 123–25, 127, 130
Chang Shih-chao, 31–32, 35, 37, 42, 111–12, 116, 137, 139
Chang T'ai-yen (see Chang Ping-lin)
Chang Tzu-p'ing, 96
Ch'ang-sha, 27, 29, 39–40, 42, 68, 71, 86, 118
Ch'ang-shou szu, 87
Chao Pai-hsien (see Chao Sheng)
Chao Sheng, 41–42
Chekiang, 24, 49, 83
Ch'en Ch'i-mei, 52, 69, 71, 83, 106, 115, 118
Ch'en Ch'ü-ping, 51, 68, 70, 72, 75, 121
Ch'en Kuo-fu, 42, 118
Ch'en Shao-pai, 30, 35–37

Ch'en Tu-hsiu, 27, 32, 34–35, 37, 41–43, 48, 61, 87, 98, 111–12, 116–17, 137
Ch'en Ying-shih (see Ch'en Ch'i-mei)
Cheng Ch'en-kung, 66
Cheng T'ung-sun, 98–99, 104
Ch'eng Yen-sheng, 128–29
Ch'eng-ch'eng Academy (see Seizo Gakko)
Ch'i-chüeh, 109, 130
Chia Pao-yü, 95
Chia-yen tsa-chih (see The Tiger)
Chiang I-an, 139
Chiang Kai-shek, 22, 118
Chiao-hsi-mo, 39, 46
Chieh-sheng (see Su Chao-ying)
Chien Chao-liang, 127
Ch'ien Hsüan-t'ung, 137
Ch'ien-t'ang, 67, 131–32
Chih-yüan ching-shê (see Jetavana School)
Chihli, 115
Childe Harold's Pilgrimage, 62
Chin Hua-chien, 34
Ch'in dynasty, 30–31, 62, 76
Ch'in Li-shan, 25, 36
Ch'in Yü-liu, 27, 29, 40
China, 15, 19, 23–24, 27, 39, 47, 49, 56, 60–61, 63, 68, 76, 83, 85, 88, 91, 107, 109, 115, 132, 139, 142
China Alliance, 44, 52, 69–71, 74, 84, 97
China Daily (The), 30, 35–37
China Guild House, 74
China Restoration Society, 40
China Revolutionary Party, 97, 99, 108, 115, 120
China Sea, 31
China Society, 140
Chinese Educational Association, 31, 69
Chinese Fiction (The), 56
"Chinese Literature of the Last Fifty Years," 137
Chinese Poetry in English Verse, 56
Chinese Repository (The), 56
Chinese Student Army, 28
Chinese Students' Anti-Russian Volunteer Corps, 28–29, 51, 71
Ching K'o, 30
Ching-an, 106
Ching-cheng, 40
Ch'ing dynasty, 38, 50, 70, 104, 141
Ch'ing-nien hui (see Youth Association)
Ch'iu Chin, 49
Ch'iu-t'ung (see Chang Shih-chao)
Chou Shu-jen, 96, 138, 140
Chou Tso-jen, 137–38
Chou Wu, 106
Chronological Life of Su Man-shu and Other Articles, 89, 122, 138
"Chronology of Byron's Life" (A), 81
Chu Shao-p'ing, 106
Chü Cheng, 108, 110, 115–16, 119–20
Ch'ü Ta-chün, 54–55
Ch'ü Weng-shan (see Ch'ü Ta-chün)
Ch'ü Yüan, 61, 73, 137
Chuang Chih, 116–17
Chuang-hsiang (Chuang-hsiang ch'u-shih), 76–78, 88
Chung-hua hui-kuan (see China Guild House)
Chung-hua kê-ming tang (see China Revolutionary Party)
Chung-kuo chiao-yü hsüeh-hui (see Chinese Educational Association)
Chung-kuo jih-pao (see The China Daily)
Chung-kuo t'ung-meng hui (see China Alliance)
Chungking, 71, 139
Cleopatra, 73
"Cloud Messenger" (The), 61
Code of Manu, 55
Cold Mountain Temple, 103
Columbia University, 108
Commercial Journal (The), 37
Communist Manifesto, 46
Communist party, 27, 70, 139
Complete Works of Man-shu (ed. Liu Ya-tzu), 89, 122, 138
Complete Works of the Reverend Man-shu (ed. Wen Kung-chih), 139
Confucianism, Confucius, 20–21, 38, 54, 127, 138
Cowper, William, 73
Creation Society, 141

Critical Biography of Su Man-shu (A), 139
Current Affairs Institute, 25
Czologosz, Leon, 32

Daily Life (The), 99
Dame aux camélias (La), 97, 141
Davis, John Francis, 56–57
Dharmapala, 60
Divine State Daily, 84
Don Juan, 62
Dream of the Red Chamber, 57, 95, 136
Dumas, Alexandre, fils, 97, 141
Dusyanta, King, 58
Dutch in Java, 85, 124
Dutt, Toru, 81

Eastwick, E. B., 57
Egypt, 61
Elder Brothers' Association, 40
Elder Ch'en-shih, 15, 17–18, 20, 89
Elementary Grammar of the Sanskrit Language (An), 46
Elizabeth, Empress, 33
"Emma Goldman, the Heroine," 32–33
Engels, Friedrich, 46
England, 15, 111
Esoteric Essences of Chinese and English Poetry, 110, 141

Fa Hsien, 79
Fa-jen, 93, 95, 135
Fan P'ang, 85
Fan-wen tien (see *Sanskrit Grammar*)
"Fantine," 34
Feng Ching-ju, 22
Feng Tzu-yu, 22, 27, 30, 35–36, 44, 74, 89, 129
Feng-hsien, 119
Fletcher, John B., 62–64, 81
Foochow Road, 105
France, 15
Francis Joseph, Emperor, 33
Franke, Otto, 60, 62–63
French Concession, 116, 119
Fu-tan University, 142
Fukien, 56, 90

Gems of Chinese Verse, 64
Germany, 60
Ghocha, 53, 55–56
Giles, Herbert A., 56
Goethe, 57–58, 73, 80–81
Goldman, Emma, 32–33, 124
Grand Magazine (The), 119
Great Republican, 84
Greece, 56, 61, 81

Haggard, H.R., 73
Hai-ch'in, 119
Hai-k'ou, 64
Hai-ning Hospital, 118
Hai-yün szu, 87
Hainan, 61
Hakone, 92
Han dynasty, 22, 110
Hangchow, 41, 43, 51, 59, 67–68, 85, 87, 93, 116, 121, 132
Hankow, 25
Hankow Road, 105
Hanoi, 36
Hawaii, 16
Heart Sutra, 47
Heaven's Bell, 84
Hebrew Old Testament, 101
Herald Wind (The), 57
Hewitt, 81
Hindustan, 80
Hirato, 66
Hishaku, 76, 82, 85–88, 95
Ho Chen, 38, 45–46, 48, 52, 123, 129
Ho Mei-shih, 35, 111–12
Hoihow (see Hai-k'ou)
Hokkaido University, 140
Hong Kong, 18, 21–23, 29–31, 33, 35–37, 57, 77, 83, 92, 94, 96, 98, 105, 113, 139
Honolulu, 22
Hopei, 115
Hsiang-shan, 16–18, 30–31, 37, 39, 44, 89
Hsiao Jen-ch'iu, 120, 122
Hsia-shuo ta-kuan (see The Grand Magazine)
Hsieh Ch'iu-yün, 111, 113
Hsin ch'ing-nien tsa-chih (see The New Youth)

Hsin Nan-shê (see New Southern Society)
Hsin-min Lane, 118
Hsing-sheng (see Vita Nuova)
Hsü Chün-mien, 21, 37
Hsü Jen-ju, 107
Hsü-t'ing (see Su Hsü-t'ing)
Hsüan-t'ung, 62
Hsüeh Meng-chu, 111–13
Hsüeh San, 106
Hsüeh-mei, 91–93, 95
Hu Chi-ch'en (see Hu Huai-ch'en)
Hu Han-min, 44–45
Hu Huai-ch'en, 89–90, 127
Hu Shih, 96, 127, 137, 140–41
Hua Hsüeh-nan, 106
Hua-hsing hui (see China Restoration Society)
Huang Chia-mu, 90
Huang Chieh, 50, 83, 127
Huang Hsing, 28–29, 40, 42, 44, 69, 71, 127
Huang Hui-wen (see Huang Chieh)
Huang K'an, 57
Huang Ming-ch'i, 139
Huang Tsung-yang, 31
Huang-shih, 15, 39
Hugo, 32–34, 141
Hui Sheng, 79
Hui-chou, 36, 87
Hui-lung szu (see Monastery of the Intelligent Dragon)
Humbert, King, 33
Hunan, 24, 40
Huns, 110
Hupei, 24, 115

I-chou, 59
I-sheng (see Shen Yen-mou)
Iizuka Akira, 90, 139–40
Ikeda Takashi, 139–40
India, 46, 48, 51, 53, 55, 59–61, 100–01, 124
Indian Classical Literature, 39, 46–47, 53, 55, 57–58, 61, 80, 94, 100–01, 110
Indigo, Mount, 103
Industrial School, 39–40, 71, 118
"Inscribed on Byron's Poetic Works," 75–76
"Inscribed on Shelley's Poetic Works," 64
International Settlement, 31–32, 84, 105–6, 118
Islam, 80, 101
"Isles of Greece" (The), 62, 64, 124, 140
Italy, 33

Japan, 15–22, 24–31, 35–39, 43–46, 49, 51, 53, 59–64, 67, 77, 79–80, 85–88, 91, 97, 100, 107–10, 115, 118, 120, 126, 132, 134, 139
Japanese Association for Sanskrit Studies, 61–62
Java, 68, 71, 79–80, 82–83, 85, 89–90, 98–100, 124
Jetavana School, 59, 61, 97, 124
Jeunesse (La) (see The New Youth)
Joffre, Rue, 118
"John Gilpin," 73
Jones, William, 58
Journal of the Southern Society, 68, 72, 78–79
Journal on Chinese Learning, 50

Kalidasa, 57–58, 61, 80, 101
Kama, 101
Kamata, 44, 67
K'ang Yu-wei, 20–21, 25, 37
K'ang-liang faction, 88
Kao Hsieh, 51
Kao Hsü, 51, 68, 70, 72, 74, 79–80
Kao T'ien-mei (see Kao Hsü)
Kawai, 15–17, 38, 43–45, 48–49, 51, 55, 85, 88–89, 91–92, 95, 110, 118, 120
Kê-lao hui (see Elder Brothers' Association)
Kiangsu, 24, 52, 83
Kingdom of the Lions (Ceylon), 80
Kobe, 37
Koxinga (see Cheng Ch'eng-kung)
Ku Hung-ming, 73
Kuang-ch'ao Cemetery, 120
Kuang-hsü, 20, 62
Kuang-tz'u Hospital, 119–20

Kuei Po-hua, 61, 97
K'ung Tzu-chen, 70
Kuo Mo-jo, 141
Kuo-hsüeh pao-ts'un hui (see Association for the Preservation of National Learning)
Kuo-hsüeh-shê (*see* Society for National Learning)
Kuo-min jih-jih pao (see National People's Daily)
Kuo-ts'ui hsüeh-pao (see Journal on Chinese Learning)
Kuomintang (see Nationalist party)
Kwangtung, 15–16, 24, 36, 39, 53–55, 59, 88, 91, 127
Kyoto, 66, 107

Lao, Mount, 116
Legge, James, 56
Lei-feng (see Thunder Peak)
Leopold II, Belgium, 33
Leung, George Kin, 90, 96
Li Cheng, 54
Li Chia-yu, 100
Li Ho, 73
Li Hsiao-tun, 60
Li Ling's letter to Su Wu, 110
Li Po, 56, 73, 110, 130, 137
Li Sao, 61
Li Shang-yin, 73, 102
Li-ch'i, 16, 23, 37, 89
Liang Ch'i-ch'ao, 22, 25, 37
Lien-hua nü-shih (see Miss Lily)
Lien-p'ei, 116–17
Lily, Miss, 64
Lin Shu, 73, 97, 141
Lin Tai-yü, 57, 95, 129
Lin Tzu-yüan, 20–21, 30–31, 44
Ling-fang, 116–17
Literary Chronicle, 139
Liu A-lan, 113–15
Liu San, 28, 41, 43–44, 51, 53, 59–61, 87, 128
Liu Shih-p'ei, 38, 42–46, 48, 51–53, 87, 98, 123, 128
Liu Wu-chi, 89, 122, 138–40
Liu Ya-tzu, 43, 68–71, 75, 83–86, 88–89, 98–99, 104, 106–7, 115, 119, 122, 124–26, 135, 138–40
Lo Fei-yü, 111–12
Lo, Irving Y.C., 141
Lo-feng (see Shen Yen-mou)
Lo-pi-shih (see Señorita Lopez)
London, 140
Lone Swan (The) (see Tale of the Lone Swan)
Longfellow, 73
Lopez, Rev., 75–76, 92, 95, 124, 140
Lopez, Señorita, 73, 75–77, 81, 96
Lu, Emma, 111
Lu Hsiang-fu, 21
Lu Hsün (see Chou Shu-jen)
Lu Lien, 30
Lu Ling-su, 128

Ma Chün-wu, 44, 83, 140
Ma Chung-shu, 126
Madhyamika Buddhism, 107
Madrid, 77–78
Mahabharata, 57, 61, 101
Mahabodhi Society, 60
Mahayana, 110
Mai Wu-ku, 111–13
"Maid of Athens," 57, 62
Man-shu (narrator in "Tale of a Broken Hairpin"), 116–17
Man-shu (see Su Man-shu)
Man-shu's Literary Remains, 122
Man-shu's Poems and Imitations of Man-shu's Poems, 139
Manchuria, 28, 98
Manchus, 15, 20, 22, 24–26, 29, 31, 36–38, 50, 52, 54, 56, 67–68, 83, 98, 124, 128, 138
Mandarin Duck and Butterfly School (of fiction), 136, 138, 142
Mandju (see Su Man-shu)
"Manifesto to Both Officials and Commoners" (A), 58–59, 124
Manjusri, Bodhisattva, 37
"Martin Luther of the Chinese Buddhist Reform Movement," 125
Marx, Karl, 46
Masuda Wataru, 139–40
May Fourth Movement, 70
Mazzini, 26
McAleavy, Henry, 76, 90, 136, 140
McKinley, William, 32

Mei-niang, 114
Meiji (reformation), 15–16
Memorial Volume of the Reverend Man-shu's Works, 139
Meng, Bishop, 34
Mercer, W. T., 56
Michel, Clemence Louise, 49
Middle Kingdom, 61–63, 103
Middle Kingdom (The), 57
Milton, 73
Min-chiang, 56
Min-ch'üan pao (see People's Right)
Min-kuo hsin-wen (see People's National News)
Min-kuo jih-pao (see The Republican Daily)
Min-kuo tsa-chih (see The Republic)
Min-li pao (see People's Stand)
Min-pao (see People's Report)
Min-sheng jih-pao (see People's Voice Daily)
Ming dynasty, 50, 54, 66
Ming Nan-tê, 34
Ming-tê School, 40
"Miscellaneous Criticism of Man-shu's Writings," 136
Miserable Society (The), 33–35
Misérables (Les), 32–34, 141
"Mission to the Western Regions," 79
Mitsukoshi department store, 139
Modern Geographical Terms and Itinerary Charts for Fa Hsien's "Records of the Buddhist Kingdoms" and Hui Sheng's "Mission to the Western Regions", 79
Mohammed, 101
Moku A Mi, 139
Momosuke, 65
Monastery of Longevity, 87
Monastery of the Intelligent Dragon, 87
Monastery of the Sea Clouds, 87
Monier-Williams, Monier, 46, 87
More Gems of Chinese Poetry, 64
Moslem Rebellion, 15
"Mountain Man of Sheng-t'ang" (The), 57
"Mourning One's Dreams on the Banks of Lake Fen," 128
Müller, Friedrich Max, 46–47, 87
Mūne-o, 88
Myriel, Charles, 34

Nagasaki, 50, 93
Names and Identifications of the Flora of the Western Hemisphere, 79
Nami-ko, 73
Nan-shê (Southern Society)
Nan-shê ts'ung-k'e (see Journal of the Southern Society)
Nan-yang Public School, 31
Nanda, 64
Nanking, 26, 31, 41–42, 52, 59, 61, 71, 83, 86, 124
Nanking Military Academy, 31
Nanking Road, 106
Napoleon I, 34–35
Nara, 107
National Peking University, 52, 142
National People's Daily, 32–35, 84, 111
Nationalist government, 22, 69
Nationalist party, 27–28, 42, 45, 70–71, 107, 121, 142
Natsume Soseki, 139
New Literature Movement, 141
New Southern Society, 70
New York, 108
New Youth (The), 116
Nien rebellion, 15
Nihonbashi, 139
"Nineteen Miscellaneous Poems Written During My Sojourn in Japan," 109–10, 115, 133–34
Niu Yung-chien, 28, 36
North Vietnam, 39
"Note to Fa-jen," 135

"Occasional Poems," 65–66, 131, 133
"Ocean" (The), 62, 94, 96
Omori, 44
"On Encountering Sorrow," 61
"On Painting the Portrait of a Harpsichord Player," 65, 134
On Service with the King, 57
Opium War, 15
Orphan Hill, West Lake, 121
Othello, 100
Owaka, 17, 89

Pacific News (The), 84–86, 88–89, 97
Pan-American Exposition, 32
Pao T'ien-hsiao, 65, 119, 139
Pao-ch'ang Road, 118
Paris, 45
"Parting from Mr. Chang at Java," 85
"Passing by Kamata," 67, 132
"Passing by the Birthplace of Cheng Ch'eng-kung," 66–67
Patriotic Student Society, 31, 69
Pei-t'ing, 69
Peking, 15, 20, 52, 60, 68
People's National News, 84
People's Report, 45, 53, 70, 87, 123
People's Right, 84
People's Stand, 84
People's Voice Daily, 84
Père Robert, Rue, 119
Picture of Dorian Gray (The), 112
"Poems to the Harpsichord Player," 65–66, 134
"Poems without Titles," 102, 133
Poetic Remains of the Swallow's Mausoleum, 126, 135
Poetry Classic, 56–57, 110
Poetry of the Chinese, 57
"Postscript to the *Voices of the Tide*," 76, 82, 85–88, 95
Practical Grammar of the Sanskrit Language (A), 46
Prajnāpāramitāhrdaya (see Heart Sutra)
"Preface to Man-shu's Painting Album," 43, 48–49
"Preface to *Voices of the Tide*," 80–82

Raskha, 106
Ramayana, 55, 57
Random Notes from a Swallow's Mausoleum, 42, 79, 98–101, 106, 108
"Records of the Buddhist Kingdoms," 79
Reform Movement, 20
Republic (The), 79, 99, 108–10, 115, 120
Republican Daily (The), 120
Resurgent China Association, 22
Revolutionary Army (The), 31
Richards, Timothy, 60
Robinson Crusoe, 73
Rome, 120
Rottauscher, Anna von, 90
Russia, 22, 28

Saburō, 76, 88, 90–96
Sakuntala, 57–58, 80–81, 101
Salomé, 112
San Francisco, 22
San-lang (see Saburō)
San-lun, 107
Sanron (see San-lun)
Sanskrit, 39, 46, 58, 61
Sanskrit Grammar, 46–47, 86–87, 120, 140
Sanskrit Grammar for Beginners (A), 46
Sanskrit Vowels and Consonants, 97
Satô Haruo, 139–40
Schopenhauer, 125
Seizo Gakko, 28
Selected Poems of Byron, 62–63, 80–82, 141
Shakespeare, 73, 100, 112
Shang dynasty, 62
Shanghai, 18–19, 23–25, 27–29, 31–35, 38–41, 43–45, 49–50, 52, 59–61, 63–64, 68–72, 78–79, 82–85, 90, 93, 97–99, 104–7, 111, 115–16, 118, 121, 129, 137, 139–40
Shanghai Famine Relief Bazaar, 86
Shansi, 115
Shantung, 115
Shao Yüan-ch'ung, 108, 115
Shelley, 64, 73, 81, 124, 141
Shen Yen-mou, 79, 98–99, 102
Shen-chou jih-pao (see Divine State Daily)
Sheng-chê, 99, 102, 104
Sheng-huo jih-pao (see The Daily Life)
Shih-ching (see Poetry Classic)
"Shih-hua," 99
Shih-pao (see Times)
Shih-wu hsüeh-t'ang (see Current Affairs Institute)
Shizuko, 91–96
Short History of Chinese Fiction, 140
Siam, 39, 77–78
Singapore, 68, 72, 75, 78
"Singing on My Way to Yodoe," 67, 132

Sino-Japanese War, 18, 138–39
Six Dynasties, 103, 110
Snowy Swan (see Señorita Lopez)
So-nosuke, 88
Society for National Learning, 39–40
Society of Heaven and Earth (see Triad Society)
"Song of Everlasting Sorrow," 56
Soochow, 35, 41, 65, 68, 70, 86, 99, 102, 104, 111
Soochow University, 26
Soul-Secluded Monastery, 41
Southern Society, 68–72, 84, 89, 97, 105, 115, 121, 127, 130–31, 137, 142
Soviet Union, 22, 28
Spain, 75, 77
Strange Stories from a Chinese Studio, 137
Su Chao-ying (see Su Chieh-sheng)
Su Chieh-sheng, 15–16, 18, 37
Su Hsü-t'ing, 15–16, 37, 89
Su Hsüan-ying (see Su Man-shu), 120
Su Man-shu:
Articles and books: "Account of My Refugee Life on the Seashores of Sala" (An), 53, 55–56, 125; "Admonishment to All Buddhist Disciples" (An), 58–59, 124; *Affinities in Literature,* 56–58, 62, 80, 110, 123, 141; "Alas! We Cantonese!", 32–33; "Emma Goldman, the Heroine," 32–33; *Esoteric Essences of Chinese and English Poetry,* 110, 141; "Manifesto to Both Officials and Commoners" (A), 58–59; *Miserable Society (The)* (Trsl.), 33–35; "Postscript to *Voices of the Tide,*" 76, 82, 85–88, 95; Preface to Chang Shih-chao's "Tale of Twin Chessboards," 111; "Preface to *Voices of the Tide*" (English), 80–82; *Random Notes from a Swallow's Mausoleum,* 42, 79, 98–101, 106, 108; *Selected Poems of Byron,* 62–63, 80–82, 141; *Tales of Spectral Splendors on the Shores of Kwangtung,* 53–54, 99; "Talk on the South Seas" (A), 85; *Voices of the Tide,* 76, 80–82, 100, 110, 141
Buddhism, 36–37, 39–40, 47, 58–59, 60–61, 66, 75, 77–79, 87, 105, 107–8, 124, 127, 142
Byron, 51, 57, 62–64, 73, 94, 96, 100, 108, 124, 133, 140–41
Chronology, 13
Education: Seizo Gakko, 28–29; Ta-t'ung School, 20–23; Waseda University, 23, 27
Fiction; "Red Tears at the End of the World," 108; "Tale of a Broken Hairpin," 116–19, 136; "Tale of Crimson Silk" (A), 111–13, 137, 139; *Tale of the Lone Swan* (A), 76, 79, 85, 88–96, 111, 135–36, 139; "Tale on the Burning of the Sword" (A), 113–15, 137, 139; "Tale that was No Dream" (The), 119
Finances, 29–30, 35, 39, 40–41, 43–44, 46, 48, 50, 77, 84, 91–92, 97, 106, 118, 122, 125–27
Health, 49–51, 73, 75, 78, 97, 105–8, 110, 115–16, 118–19, 122
Indian Classical Literature, 39, 46, 53, 55, 57–58, 61, 80, 94, 100–1
Letters: to Chuang-hsiang, 76; Hsü Jen-ju, 107; Kao T'ien-mei, 72, 74; Liu San, 43, 51, 53, 60–61, 87; Liu Ya-tzu, 75, 83, 107, 115, 119, 125; Ma Chün-wu, 83; Shao Yüan-ch'ung, 108; Teng Meng-shih, 108; Teng Sheng-hou, 87; Ts'ai Shou, 83
Paintings, 39, 41–43, 48, 63, 123, 128–129
Parentage, 15–18, 37, 88–89, 140
Poems: "Bidding Farewell to T'ang Kuo-tun with Two Poems and a Painting," 30, 32; "Inscribed on Byron's Poetic Works," 75–76; "Inscribed on Shelley's Poetic Works," 64; "Nineteen Miscellaneous Poems Written During My Sojourn in Japan," 109–10, 115, 133–34; "Note to Fa-jen," 135; "Occasional Poems," 65–66,

131, 133; "On Painting the Portrait of a Harpsichord Player," 65, 134; "Parting from Mr. Chang at Java," 85; "Passing by Kamata," 67, 132; "Passing by the Birthplace of Cheng Ch'eng-Kung," 66–67; Poems to the Harpsichord Player, 65–66, 134; "Poems without Titles," 102, 133; "Singing on My Way to Yodoe," 67, 132; "Title Lost," 134; "To Ch'en Tu-hsiu as I Pass by Wakamatsucho in a State of Emotion," 131; "To Liu San at Nanking," 53; "Written During My Stay at White Clouds Monastery at West Lake," 41, 132; "Written in Soochow, Using the Rhymes in I-sheng's Poems," 102–104

Relation with Kawai, 15–17, 38, 43–45, 48–49, 51, 55, 85, 88–89, 110, 118, 120

Revolutionary activities: Association for the People's Military Education, 28–29; Chinese Students' Anti-Russian Volunteer Corps, 28–29, 51, 71; Threat to kill K'ang Yu-wei, 37; Youth Association, 26–27; see also 38, 40, 46, 53, 61, 83

Sanskrit, 39, 46, 58, 61

Teaching: Anhwei High School, An-ch'ing, 97–99, 129; Army Elementary School, Nanking, 41; China Guild House, Surabaya, Java, 74–75; Ching-cheng School, Ch'ang-sha, 40; Industrial School, Ch'ang-sha, 39–40, 71; Jetavana School, Nanking, 59, 61, 97, 124; Ming-tê School, Ch'ang-sha, 40, 42; School in Soochow, 35, 41, 119; Wan-chiang School, Wu-hu, 42–43, 98; Young Men's Association, Bangkok, 39

Translations, 53, 55–56, 61–62, 73, 76–77, 79–82, 101, 125, 140–41

Works, lost: *Botanic Treatise on the Flora of the Western Hemisphere (A)*, or *Names and Identifications of the Flora of the Western Hemisphere* (with Lo-feng), 79; *Modern Geographical Terms and Itinerary Charts for Fa Hsien's "Records of the Buddhist Kingdoms" and Hui Sheng's "Missions to the Western Regions,"* 79; *Sanskrit Grammar*, 46–47, 86–87, 120, 140; *Sanskrit Vowels and Consonants*, 97; *Swallow's Letter (The)* (English trsl.), 76–77

Writings about: by Chang Ping-lin, 125, 127; Chou Tso-jen, 137–38; [in] *History of Chinese Literature* (by Chinese Department students, Fu-tan University), 142; *History of Chinese Literature* (by Chinese Department students, National Peking University), 142; Ho Chen, 129; Hsiao Jen-ch'iu, 122; Hu Shih, 137, 141; Huang Ming-ch'i, 139; Iizuka Akira, 139–40; Kawai, 43, 48–49; Liu Wu-chi and Liu Ya-tzu, 89, 122, 126, 135, 138–40; Lo, Irving Y.C., 141; Ma Chung-shu, 126; McAleavy, Henry, 90, 140; Sato Haruo, 139–40; Ts'ai Shou, 41; Woon, Ramon, 141; Yonezawa Hideo, 140; Yü Ta-fu, 136

Su Man-shu, a Sino-Japanese Genius, 90, 140

"Su Man-shu's Life and Works," 140

"Su Man-shu's Poetry Album," 139

Su San-lang (see Su Man-shu), 88

Su Shao-ch'iung, 138

Su Shao-hsien, 89

Su Shih, 130

Su Shih-ch'ang, 89

Su Wei-han, 23, 84

Su Wei-lu, 89

Su-pao, 31–32

Sui-pi, 99

Sun Yat-sen, 16, 44, 69–71, 83, 85, 99, 108, 115–16, 121–22, 127, 142

Sung Chiao-jen, 44–45, 70, 84, 98–99, 106–7, 115

Sung dynasty, 57, 70, 99, 129–30

Surabaya, 68, 72, 74, 80, 83, 86, 101

Sutra Press, 59
Swallow's Letter (The), 76–77
Swallow's Mausoleum, 121
Sweden, 33
T'ai-yen (see Chang Ping-lin)
Ta kung-huo pao (see Great Republican)
Ta-ch'eng ch'i-hsin lu, 60
Ta-t'ung Advanced Institute, 22, 25
Ta-t'ung School, 20–21, 87, 110, 129
Tada-o, 88
Tai Chi-t'ao, 108, 115
Tai-yün, 106
T'ai-p'ing Rebellion, 15
T'ai-p'ing-yang pao (see The Pacific News)
T'ai-yen (see Chang Ping-lin)
Taipei, 139
Taiwan, 67, 139, 142
"Tale of a Broken Hairpin," 116–19, 136
"Tale of Crimson Silk" (A), 111–13, 137, 139
Tale of the Lone Swan (A), 76, 79, 85, 88–96, 111, 135–36, 139
"Tale of Twin Chessboards" (A), 111
"Tale on the Burning of the Sword" (A), 113–15, 137, 139
"Tale that was No Dream" (The), 119
Tales of Shakespeare, 73
Tales of Spectral Splendors on the Shores of Kwangtung, 53–54, 99
"Talk on the South Seas" (A), 85
T'an-luan, 111–13
T'ang dynasty, 64, 70, 99, 104, 110, 130–31
T'ang Ts'ai-ch'ang, 25
T'ao Ch'ien, 100, 110
Tê-shan, 59
Teng Ch'iu-mei (see Teng Shih)
Teng Meng-shih, 108, 109
Teng Sheng-hou, 87, 98
Teng Shih, 50
Tennyson, 73
Thailand, 39, 77–78
"Three Hundred Poems Without Title," 102
Thunder Peak, 41, 87, 132
Tien Yee News, 45–46, 56, 88, 123
T'ien T'ung, 108, 115
T'ien-i pao (see Tien Yee News)
T'ien-to pao (see Heaven's Bell)
Tientsin, 25
Tiger (The), 110–11, 113
Tiger Hill, 68
Times, 84
"To Ch'en Tu-hsiu as I Pass by "Wakamatsu-cho in a State of Emotion," 131
"To Liu San at Nanking," 53
Tokutomi Kenjiro, 139
Tokyo, 15–16, 22–26, 29, 32, 36, 40, 44–46, 50–51, 56, 61–62, 71, 80, 87–88, 90, 97, 99, 107, 110–11, 139
Triad Society, 49
True Story of Ah Q, 96
"True Su Man-shu" (The), 140
Ts'ai Shou, 41, 63–64, 70, 83, 115, 123
Ts'ai Yüan-pei, 31, 43, 52
Ts'an shê-hui (see The Miserable Society)
Tsing Hua University, 98
Tsingtao, 115–16
Tsou Yung, 31–32, 84
Tu Fu, 73, 100, 110, 130
Tu-ku Ts'an, 113–15
T'ung-hua, 106
T'ung-Kuang School (of poetry), 70
Tzu-hsi, Empress Dowager, 20
Tzu-ku (see Su Man-shu), 88

Uēno, 87
United States (of America), 16, 108

Valjean, Jean, 34
Vallon, Rue, 116
Vancouver, 22
Vita Nuova, 140
Voice of the Tide, 76, 80–82, 100, 110, 141
Volunteer Corps (see Chinese Students' Anti-Russian Volunteer Corps)

Wan-chiang School, 42–43, 98
Wang Chao-ming, 44–45, 120–21
Wang Ching-wei (see Wang Chao-ming)

Wang Ta-hsieh, 29–30
Waseda University, 22–23, 27, 87, 110, 129
Wei-hsiang, 119
Wen Kung-chih, 139
Wen-hsüeh yin-yüan (see Affinities in Literature)
Weng-shan (see Ch'ü Weng-shan)
West Lake, 41, 43, 59, 94, 121, 132
"What Kind of Person was Su Man-shu?", 139–40
White Clouds Monastery, 41, 59, 132
"Who Presented Me with a Volume of Shelley's Melodious Verses?", 64
Wilde, Oscar, 112
William II (Germany), 33
Williams, Samuel S., 57
"Without Title," 102
Women's Stories by Weng-shan, 55
Wonderful Brushworks of the Reverend Man-shu, 123
Woon, Ramon, 141
Woosung Arsenal, 83
"Written During My Stay at White Clouds Monastery at West Lake," 41, 132
"Written in Soochow, Using the Rhymes in I-sheng's Poems," 102–4
Wu, 102–3
Wu Ching-heng, 31
Wu-han, 83
Wu-hsi, 27
Wu-hu, 42–44, 86
Wunde Schwan (Der), 90

Yang Jen-shan (see Yang Wen-hui)
Yang Wen-hui, 59–61, 97, 124
Yangtze, 15, 24–25, 68, 83
Yeh Ch'u-ts'ang, 84, 106, 120, 128
Yeh Lan, 27–28, 39–40
Yellow Dragon, 21
Yellow Flower Mound uprising, 42
Yen Fu, 73, 141
Yi River, 30
Yodoe, 67
Yokohama, 15, 17–22, 26, 30, 33, 44, 51, 72, 79, 88, 92, 94, 129
Yonezawa Hideo, 139–40
Young Men's Association, Bangkok, 39
Younger Ch'en-shih, 15
Youth Association, Tokyo, 26
Yü Ta-fu, 96, 136–37
Yü-luan, 111
Yü-ssu Weekly, 138
Yüan dynasty, 104, 129
Yüan Shih-k'ai, 52, 69, 71, 85, 98–99, 107, 115
Yung-lo Street, 36
Yunnan, 116

Zushi, 51, 92